FEARDOM

HOW POLITICIANS EXPLOIT YOUR EMOTIONS AND WHAT YOU CAN DO TO STOP THEM

CONNOR BOYACK

Libertas Press
Salt Lake City, Utah

Libertas Press
785 E. 200 S., Suite 2
Lehi, UT 84043

Feardom: How Politicians Exploit Your Emotions
and What You Can Do to Stop Them / Connor Boyack — 1st ed.

Cover design by Elijah Stanfield.
Cover image source: Copyright © Hiro Oshima 2001. Reproduced with permission.

ISBN-13: 978-0-9892912-6-2 (paperback)
ISBN-13: 978-0-9892912-7-9 (e-book)
Second printing: November 2016.

For bulk orders, send inquiries to: info@libertasutah.org

ADDITIONAL PRAISE

"Good journalism should be skeptical of government actions and should inform and empower individuals. Most media institutions fall short of this ideal and instead routinely paralyze their viewers with fear. As Connor Boyack explains in this compelling book, the consequences of this are drastic and detrimental—but they are not irreversible. *Feardom* offers solutions to this problem that are sorely needed and very timely. A must read!"

> —**Ben Swann**, award-winning investigative journalist

"Forget sex—what really sells is fear. And at last, here's a book that follows the fear as surely and shockingly as Bob Woodward and Carl Bernstein followed the money. The only thing to fear is people not reading *Feardom* itself."

> —**Lenore Skenazy**, author of *Free-Range Kids, How to Raise Safe, Self-Reliant Children (Without Going Nuts with Worry)*

"*Feardom* explains clearly and succinctly how Americans have lost their freedom and what they need to do to win it back. Everyone should read this book."

> —**Jacob Hornberger**, founder and president, The Future of Freedom Foundation

DEDICATION

To all those in my life who helped me find the red pill.

CONTENTS

FOREWORD

by Tom Woods

WE ARE TOLD THAT what makes our system great is that we make political decisions through rational discussion, not the arbitrary fiat of the kings of yore. But in fact, the last thing the state wants is calm deliberation. It thrives on fear. Government power tends to expand no matter what, to be sure, but it expands much more rapidly under what are perceived as emergency conditions. Give us more power, citizen! There's no time to lose!

Government officials push this line because they know that power once granted is almost never relinquished. All they need to do is trick the public into accepting the latest rationale for additional rounds of government expansion. The people may later repent of their haste in consenting to this episode of government growth, but these second thoughts rarely amount to full-fledged campaigns of repeal, especially since they'd be up against the power and institutional inertia of entrenched bureaucracy, which rarely yields ground.

The exploitation of the public through fear is not limited to left or right. It is common to both sides of what we laughingly call our political spectrum. The left spins tales of wicked businessmen, who without the benevolent hand of government would lord it over the rest of us, and who would churn out poison sandwiches and exploding computer monitors. The right warns us of foreign malefactors who have no rational motivations or identifiable grievances. They wish only to pursue evil, we are told, and they attack the United States not because of anything the U.S. government has done, but simply out of envy at the sheer awesomeness of the American people. (The establishment left gets in on this act, too, having in fact supported every major American war since World War I.)

When it comes to war, our political class has given us no reason not to be skeptical of its breathless claims. Few major American wars have not relied for their popular appeal on some deliberately cultivated falsehood. A few recent examples might include the alleged Gulf of Tonkin incident (Vietnam), babies being tossed out of incubators (Iraq I), "genocide" (Kosovo, where "hundreds of thousands" of dead turned out to be 2000 dead on both sides of a civil war combined), weapons of mass destruction (Iraq II), and many others besides. Tony Blair warned that Saddam Hussein's unmanned drones could reach the United Kingdom within 45 minutes. Saddam's entire drone program turned out to be a single prototype of plywood and string. But the story served its purpose: to "get Saddam," a two-bit nobody that no Westerner in his right mind had been concerned about just ten minutes earlier.

The two sides came together in the Panic of 2008 to push through all manner of ill-conceived bailouts, which we know in retrospect—as if we didn't know it at the time—made no sense. For example, normal bankruptcy proceedings for AIG would not have destroyed the economy or sent Main Street banks reeling, as we were solemnly assured it would. Main Street banks had zero exposure to the credit-default swap problem facing AIG. Had anyone bothered to check, they would have found that a grand total of about a dozen financial institutions around the world would have taken a hit. The combined capitalization of those dozen firms was $20 trillion. The loss they would have taken was in the neighborhood of $60 billion—a few months' worth of bonuses, in other words.

No wonder the political class insisted there was no time for us to look closely at these deals.

Now this episode was a little different: it was not a case of using the public's fear to stampede the people into granting still more power to the federal government. The public was in fact overwhelmingly opposed to the bailouts, a sentiment to which the flood of angry phone calls to congressional offices provided ample testimony. Instead, the political establishment chided the public for not being appropriately fearful, and went on to carry out government policy based on fear they insisted the people should have had. Yes, yes, we're sorry we have to do this, the official line ran, and we're sorry we have to do it so quickly and without deliberation, and we're sorry we have to ignore your opinions, but trust us: this is really scary, and although we'd prefer not to put it this way, you stupid rubes are too simple to understand the terrible danger involved.

In general, government cultivates fear among the public and, in turn, exploits that fear on behalf of increases in its own power. Connor Boyack examines this process in a sophisticated and compelling way in this valuable book. But he does more than simply identify the problem. He explains how to thwart government's use of fear, and how we can keep our heads as government tries to send us into a panic. If these lessons are absorbed, the next time government sets out to expand its power in light of some crisis, it won't be able to play Americans like a fiddle.

INTRODUCTION

*"Timid men... prefer the calm of despotism to
the tempestuous sea of liberty."*[1]
—Thomas Jefferson

A T THE BRINK OF WAR with France in 1798, the U.S.
Congress passed a collection of laws referred to as the Alien
and Sedition Acts. Described by their Federalist proponents
as "war measures," the Democratic-Republican opponents saw them
as unconstitutional and indefensible. While each of the four laws was
claimed to be a response to escalating tensions with France, they were
mostly a political weapon to be used against members of the minority
(Democratic-Republican) party.

One of the laws, the Naturalization Act, increased the time
immigrants had to wait for citizenship and voting rights from 5 to 14
years. As immigrants tended to favor Thomas Jefferson's Democratic-
Republican party (commonly referred to simply as Republicans), the
Federalist intent of this law was to minimize the growth, and therefore
the power, of the opposition. As one Federalist said in congressional
debate, "[I do] not wish to invite hordes of... the turbulent and
disorderly of all parts of the world, to come here with a view to

disturb our tranquility, after having succeeded in the overthrow of their own governments."[2]

Two of the four laws, the Alien Enemies Act and the Alien Friends Act, purportedly granted authority to the president to deport an alien who was either deemed dangerous or who was from a country at war with the United States. The worst of the four laws, the Sedition Act, criminalized speech by punishing any person who wrote or printed "false, scandalous and malicious writing" against Congress or the president that meant to "defame... or to bring them, or either of them, into contempt or disrepute; or to excite against them... the hatred of the good people of the United States..."[3] (Notably, the Sedition Act did not punish such speech against the vice president, Thomas Jefferson, who was not a Federalist.) President John Adams signed the Acts into law on June 14, nine years to the day after the French Revolution began.

Understanding the controversy behind these laws requires a bit of context and helps set the stage for the subject we'll be discussing in this book. Political parties were a new development in American politics, and deep divisions quickly emerged as various factions in the government rallied around the important issues of the day. While domestic differences created contention between the Federalist and Democratic-Republican parties, nothing made their blood boil like foreign affairs. Though citizens of a new, independent nation, Americans remained interested in—and greatly affected by—European politics. The Federalists sided with Britain in its conflict against France, as they were worried about the mob rule they saw rising out of the ashes of France's former monarchical system and the radical ideas that tended to germinate from such political chaos. On the other hand, Republicans favored the French and supported their newfound ideals of *liberté, égalité, fraternité*. They saw in France echoes of America's own fight for freedom.

With control of Congress and the presidency, the Federalists took advantage of their political power to crack down on their enemies and ensure that France's influence would be minimized in America. But rather than targeting and deporting French immigrants accused of insurrection, Federalists focused on their political rivals who were perceived to be sympathetic towards—if not outwardly supportive of—France's ideals and methods. Under the assumed authority of the Alien and Sedition Acts, federal officials arrested twenty-five men, most of whom were editors of Republican newspapers.

Matthew Lyon, a Republican congressman from Vermont, became the first person to be put on trial under the Sedition Act. Lyon had written a letter published in the paper for which he was an editor, criticizing Adams' "continued grasp for power."[4] A federal grand jury indicted Lyon for intentionally stirring up hatred against the president. He was later sentenced by a Federalist judge to four months in jail and a $1,000 fine, having been convicted by the jury (assembled from Vermont towns that were Federalist strongholds) for expressing seditious words with "bad intent."[5] Among those arrested was the grandson of Benjamin Franklin, who worked as the editor of the *Philadelphia Democrat-Republican Aurora*, and who was charged with libeling President Adams and thus encouraging sedition among his readers. Thomas Cooper, editor of the *Sunbury and Northumberland Gazette*, was likewise indicted for sedition, fined $400, and made to serve six months in jail. Criticism of the government had become treason against the United States.

Many themes can be observed in the events of 1798: national security in a fledgling nation; partisan rivalry among men who had previously fought side by side in the American Revolution; the destabilizing influence of a heavy influx of immigrants; and the impact of foreign affairs on American politics. However, another (less discernible) theme merits special attention, as it pervaded the political process prior to, during, and after the enactment of the Alien and Sedition Acts: fear.

As David McCullough writes in his biography of John Adams, "There was rampant fear of the enemy within"[6] during this era. For

Federalists, that enemy was French immigrants whose very existence suggested the potential for French Revolution spillover into America. Republicans, on the other hand, considered the Federalists the real "enemy within," fearing increased government power with its corresponding centralization and likely abuse. In some cases, fear was a natural and reasonable response to chaotic circumstances. But in other ways, fear was manufactured by influential individuals hoping to consolidate power and enact a desired policy.

To be sure, uncertainty permeated the political process in America's early years. The very real threat of attack on the budding nation gave urgency to settling the controversy over national security issues. Interestingly, although the United States of America has emerged from her early days of extreme vulnerability to become a world superpower, the theme of fear seems as ever-present today as it was back then. As John Adams himself once wrote, "Fear is the foundation of most governments."[7] Some things, it seems, never change.

Fear is simply part of the human condition—a motivating influence upon our thoughts and actions. Its emotional irrationality leads otherwise intelligent people to abandon logic and wisdom; as Edmund Burke once said, "No passion so effectually robs the mind of all its powers of acting and reasoning as fear."[8] It incapacitates its victim, encouraging him to fecklessly submit to others' proposed solutions. These supposed solutions are often offered by conniving conspirators looking to capitalize on the individual's defenselessness, much like a predator inducing a temporary state of paralysis in its prey. Rather than acting, the fearful person is acted upon.

For this reason, despots and authoritarians have historically studied and utilized this raw emotion to pursue their goals. Political campaigns are built upon fear. Propaganda can't work without it. The centralization of power is a natural extension of it. When Adams referred to fear as the foundation of most governments, it was not merely a rhetorical flourish. Even the primary role of government— physical protection of the citizenry—implies the fear of future attack.

As the state has grown, and as political power has concentrated, entire groups of people are motivated to action on any given issue, whether at the ballot box or protesting in the streets, using fear.

Rahm Emanuel, then White House Chief of Staff, stated in a 2008 interview, "You don't ever want a crisis to go to waste; it's an opportunity to do important things that you would otherwise avoid."[9] Crises generate fear of the unknown and of the future, and Emanuel's observation highlights the political expediency of taking advantage of such situations to advance policies that people would likely reject, absent such fear.

Conservatives predictably erupted in feigned horror at Emanuel's statement, shocked that the "left" could dare use this tactic to their political advantage. "Who's out there saying [what Emanuel said]?" asked Glenn Beck. "Is it Russia, is it Venezuela, is it the Middle East, is it extremists, is it anarchists here in America, is it the United Nations, is it our own progressives here in America that would like to overturn much of the Constitution, that would like to change America into a socialistic state?"[10] To Rush Limbaugh, Emanuel was "talking about agenda items of the Democrat Party… He's talking about himself, his party, the Democrat Party and their agenda. He's not talking about you."[11]

These and other conservative pundits and politicians united together in asserting that such an audacious strategy is relegated only to the "Chicago-style" politics of the progressive left. Though uncharacteristically frank, Emanuel's acknowledgment should not come as a shock, nor should it be seen as something belonging only to one political group. As this book will explain, individuals exploiting crises—whether spontaneous or manufactured—is a commonplace occurrence. As the sociologist David Altheide has explained, "Fear does not just happen; it is socially constructed and then manipulated by those who seek to benefit."[12]

Who stands to gain from manipulating the masses through fear? Many businessmen exploit fear in markets to increase profits and drive competitors into the ground. Some religious leaders find fear a useful tool to encourage submission and loyalty. War profiteers increase their bottom line when politicians exaggerate threats to security. Even domineering spouses or playground bullies rely upon the fear of their victims to gain control. In short, anybody seeking power over another person finds fear a useful tool, and it is for that very reason that politicians stand to gain so much through its use.

Because fear is universal, and because it is so often used by power-seeking individuals in government, those who oppose the state's interference in their lives must recognize, understand, and counteract it. To the extent that people allow their fears to affect their political opinions and corresponding actions, they will increasingly enable the very people who exploit that state of fear to gain control. Freedom shrinks with each new crisis exploited by the ruling class. Any person interested in preserving freedom must rationally study the issues on their merits. More importantly, we must persuade others to recognize the pattern of fear that pervades politics, whether in the policies themselves or in the arguments used to justify them.

Manufactured fear is a societal plague, and there have been widespread casualties. We need an antidote, since few have been properly inoculated against its devastating impact. The intent of this book is to offer the needed immunization—helping you, the reader, to recognize and reject fear so you can become free.

NOTES

1. Letter to M. Mazzei, Minerva (New York: 1791).

2. Joseph M. Lynch, *Negotiating the Constitution: The Earliest Debates Over Original Intent* (Ithaca: Cornell University, 1999), 177.

3. Edwin Williams, ed., *The Book of the Constitution* (New York: Peter Hill, 1833), 72.

4. House of Representatives, *Volume of Speeches Delivered in Congress, 1840* (Washington: Globe Office, 1840).

5. Zechariah Chafee, Jr., *Freedom of Speech in War Times* (Washington: Government Printing Office, 1919), 16.

6. David McCullough, *John Adams* (New York: Simon & Schuster, 2001), 505.

7. George A. Peek, Jr., ed., *The Political Writings of John Adams: Representative Selections* (Indianapolis: Hackett Publishing Company, Inc., 2003), 85.

8. James Prior, ed., *The Works of The Right Honorable Edmund Burke, vol. 1* (London: Bell & Sons, 1886), 88.

9. "Obama, Assembling Team, Turns to the Economy," *New York Times*, November 7, 2008, http://www.nytimes.com/2008/11/07/us/politics/07obama.html.

10. "Glenn Beck – Emanuel: 'You never want a serious crisis to go to waste'," GlennBeck.com, November 21, 2008, http://www.glennbeck.com/content/articles/article/198/18490?sid=198&elid=18490&PAGEN_5=410.

11. "Set Americans Free, Democrats! Follow the Wal-Mart Example," RushLimbaugh.com, Nov. 21, 2008, http://www.rushlimbaugh.com/daily/2008/11/21/set_americans_free_democrats_follow_the_wal_mart_example.

12. D.L. Altheide, *Creating Fear: News and the Construction of Crisis* (New York: Aldine De Gruyter), 24.

WHAT IS FEAR?

"Nothing is so much to be feared as fear."[1]
—*Henry David Thoreau*

FEAR, LIKE OTHER EMOTIONS, is often difficult to describe in words. Those who have profoundly experienced an emotion understand it better than others who lack that personal insight. Just as an elderly, devoted wife who has lived a joyful life with her husband will understand what love is better than her newlywed granddaughter, fear is something that is best understood through experience. While some emotions are felt sporadically, such as anger, loneliness, or excitement, others are more consistent in our lives. Fear tends to fall into this latter category.

At its core, fear is a biological response. A stressful stimulus induces a chain reaction that ends with a release of chemicals in the brain, causing an accelerated heartbeat, rapid breathing, and an infusion of adrenaline—the so-called "fight-or-flight" response. This reaction is automatic, and it exists to help us detect danger and maximize our probability of survival. In raw terms, fear is an information transfer; sensory organs in our body transmit signals to the brain to be processed and acted upon. First, the signal is sent to the thalamus—the brain's "switchboard"—which routes data to different areas for processing. From there, the signal is split and sent to two locations: the amygdala, serving as the brain's "threat detection" center; and the neocortex, which handles sensory perception, spatial reasoning, and conscious thought. The amygdala determines whether the signal from the stimuli matches an experience that person has had, that would suggest that it is indeed a fight-or-flight situation. For example, if the individual had a frightening run-in with a spider as a young child, an encounter with a black widow would match the previous experience and signal the amygdala that a threat exists. If there is a match, then the brain initiates the fight-or-flight response and overrides the slower signal still being sent to, and processed by, the neocortex. Should the amygdala determine that the stimuli is not a valid threat, the neocortex will instead process the signal and produce a rational reaction.

Daniel Goleman, in his 1996 book *Emotional Intelligence,* calls this process an "amygdala hijack." Reporting on the research conducted by Dr. Joseph E. LeDoux, director of the Center for the Neuroscience of Fear and Anxiety, Goleman explains how emotional reactions can override otherwise rational behavior:

> LeDoux's work revealed how the architecture of the brain gives the amygdala a privileged position as an emotional sentinel, able to hijack the brain. His research has shown that sensory signals from eye or ear travel first in the brain to the thalamus, and then—across a single synapse—to the amygdala; a second signal from the thalamus is routed to the neocortex—the thinking brain. This branching allows the amygdala to begin to respond *before* the neocortex, which mulls information through several levels of brain circuits before it fully perceives and finally initiates its more finely tailored response.

LeDoux's research is revolutionary for understanding emotional life because it is the first to work out neural pathways for feelings that bypass the neocortex. Those feelings that take the direct route through the amygdala include our most primitive and potent; this circuit does much to explain the power of emotion to overwhelm rationality.[2]

That last part is key: "the power of emotion to overwhelm rationality." To be rational is to operate based on what is true, in pursuit of an objective. Rationality requires us to fairly assess evidence in order to reach a logical conclusion. If a person encountered a spider creeping along the floor he would, if acting rationally, take appropriate steps to either avoid, capture, or kill the spider. Unfortunately, powerful emotions often overwhelm this option and lead the person to act hysterically, amplifying the perception of the level of danger that actually exists.

Let's not kid ourselves—we are not consistently rational creatures. Unlike a cold, calculating cyborg, we are influenced and enriched by our emotions, which help us to express ourselves and to find enjoyment in the world around us. Without the emotion of happiness, for example, being warm, safe, and well fed would not produce a sense of pleasure. A kiss without emotion is merely the touching of lips, but the accompanying emotions turn this physical contact into a meaningful experience. As a result, we make certain decisions, such as continuing the kiss, escalating the level of intimacy, choosing to continue spending time with the other person, and so on. Emotions not only enrich our lives, but they affect our behavior— both positively and negatively. For instance, grief over the death of a loved one could produce bitterness and reclusiveness, or it could inspire charitable and productive actions in honor of the deceased. In fact, some scientists believe that emotion is *necessary* to the decision-making process itself.

The odd story of Phineas Gage illustrates this point. As a railroad worker in the Vermont countryside in 1848, 25-year-old Gage was a model employee, deemed "efficient and capable" by his boss. He was reportedly smart, temperate, and "persistent in executing his plans of action."[3] Gage was tasked with setting explosives in rock after drilling a hole, placing gunpowder and a fuse inside, and then covering it with sand. Finally, the sand would be packed down with a three-foot long, 13-pound iron bar. Distracted by somebody calling his name one day, Gage dropped the bar into a hole that had powder and a fuse, but no sand. The material ignited and exploded, shooting the iron bar upward like a rocket, directly into Gage's face. It penetrated his left cheek, went through the top of his skull, and landed around 100 feet away, along with a portion of Gage's head.

Gage survived, and while still conscious was taken to a doctor. In less than two months the doctors deemed him "cured." Though his wounds had healed, and he could physically function like a normal person, Gage was not the same person as before. He was so different that his employers refused to take him back, and friends noted that "Gage was no longer Gage." He could not manage his emotions, and was now profane, disturbed, and impatient. He acted on his desires without any restraint. Gage was sometimes stubborn, and at other times he couldn't make up his mind. He was unable to plan for the future, and consequently drifted from job to job, eventually joining the circus as a freak, posing with the iron bar from his accident.

Researchers in the 1990s created computer simulations of Gage's skull and discovered that the accident had damaged his prefrontal cortex—a portion of the neocortex—which impaired his ability to plan and make decisions. The inability to process certain kinds of emotion greatly affected Gage's decision-making process, preventing him from accounting for, and acting upon, important data about his environment. His experience suggests that while emotion may make us irrational at times, such as during a fearful experience, its absence is a detriment to the decision-making process.

Like other emotions, fear can be positive and negative. Rational fear is effectively a time-saver, producing an automatic response during a dangerous circumstance. In such a setting, we don't want to have to reanalyze everything every time—we just want to capture or kill the spider as quickly as possible! Irrational fear, however, might drive us to jump up on a stool and scream, or it might paralyze us, allowing the spider to escape.

We see a similar result as it relates to terrorism, for example. While terrorist acts definitely occur, some of the policies enacted to prevent them are clearly irrational. In America, your chance of being killed by a terrorist is about one in 20 million. In comparison, your annual risk of dying in a car accident is 1 in 19,000; drowning in a bathtub is 1 in 800,000; dying in a building fire is 1 in 99,000; and being struck by lightning is 1 in 5,500,000. In other words, you are four times more likely to be struck by lightning than killed by a terrorist—and yet we don't expend billions of dollars on preventative measures to minimize the threat of lightning strikes.

When the evidence does not substantiate the threat—when there's no rational reason to produce a heightened emotional response and change your behavior to avoid danger—then the fear is irrational. It's rational to duck when somebody points a gun at you. It's not rational to do so when the person is making a "gun" with their fingers.

THE FEAR OF FEAR

There are many things to be legitimately afraid of. The world is admittedly a dangerous place. But modern society has mitigated many threats through measures such as pest control, sanitation and hygiene, preparedness for natural disasters, and disease prevention. Moreover, through the division of labor, we have come to rely upon individuals with specialized training in cases of extreme danger; it's comforting for most people to know that calling 911 will bring needed help.

Imagine living in a Middle Eastern country, where you might live every minute of every day in a state of fear. You may worry about starvation, or sickness, or even bombs and gunfire. It's impossible to imagine for those who haven't experienced it. No video game or feature film can come close to conveying the emotions felt in such an environment. Living in a first world nation means access to health care, a relative abundance of food, and physical safety. We simply cannot comprehend the fear that is part of many people's daily lives.

The attack on 9/11 offers a glimpse, but not for the reason you might think. Ponder for a moment where you were when you heard the news that the World Trade Center was attacked. I was 19 years old at the time, staying at my parent's home in San Diego, California. I walked in to see my mother glued to the TV, jaw slightly dropped. "Oh my gosh, oh my gosh, oh my gosh," she repeated. She was unable to process what had happened, and simply pointed to the looping video she was watching, suggesting I do the same.

What I saw looked more like computer-generated graphics from a movie than real life. Could something like this really happen in America, I wondered? As the minutes turned into hours, reporters simply regurgitated what little they knew in as many different ways as they could, cycling through what little footage they had. We were collectively dumbfounded, aghast that an attack on American soil could occur. I was sad, but I was also angry. I wanted revenge, even though I was safe in San Diego. My life was not threatened; there was no indication whatsoever that what had happened on the East Coast would be replicated in the West. I was sitting in a comfortable home, having just eaten breakfast. Outside, the birds were still chirping, and the sky looked the same as it always had. Though nothing threatened me personally, I was still profoundly affected by the news. Why?

While I wasn't afraid of an attack in San Diego, I was afraid of something. Only years later did I come to realize that I was afraid of being afraid. This new experience was unlike anything I had ever encountered. It was unusual to worry about plane attacks, anthrax, dirty bombs, and the like. I didn't like how it made me feel. It wasn't that I had a rational fear of a legitimate physical threat—I had a fear of fear.

The attack on 9/11 was a localized event, affecting only a relatively small number of Americans. As indicated earlier, the general threat of terrorism, even factoring in the large death toll on that tragic day, produces a statistically insignificant threat to the average person's life. People across the country, however, were gripped with fear. And because we are an object-oriented people, most felt the need to project that fear onto something. Some people stopped flying in airplanes, worried about a repeat attack—and for years afterward, air travel always dipped on the anniversary of 9/11.[4] Of course, this was and is an irrational fear; it is safer to travel by plane than by car. According to the National Safety Council, in 2010 there were over 22,000 passenger deaths involving automobiles, while no one died in scheduled airline travel that year.[5]

Nevertheless, Congress responded by rushing through the USA PATRIOT Act six weeks after 9/11—a 240-plus page bill that was previously written, not available to the public prior to the vote, and barely available to the elected officials in Congress, none of whom read it through before casting their votes.[6]

Two weeks previous to the bill's passage, President Bush had announced the establishment of the Office of Homeland Security to "develop and coordinate the implementation of a comprehensive national strategy to secure the United States from terrorist threats or attacks." He explained that "[t]he Office will coordinate the executive branch's efforts to detect, prepare for, prevent, protect against, respond to, and recover from terrorist attacks within the United States."[7] The office's efforts culminated in the creation of the Department of Homeland Security (DHS) one year later as a result of the Homeland Security Act of 2002. This law consolidated executive branch organizations related to "homeland security" into a single Cabinet department; twenty-two total agencies became part of this new apparatus.

The government, responding to the outcry from a fearful citizenry, was eager to "do something." All of this (and much, much more), affecting all Americans, because of a localized event materially affecting only a few. But while the event directly impacted only a small percentage of the population, its impact was felt throughout the entire country.

Seventy years earlier, responding to the Depression that affected a much higher percentage of the citizenry, Franklin D. Roosevelt asserted his "firm belief that the only thing we have to fear is fear itself—nameless, unreasoning, unjustified terror…"[8] It's a popular quote, but he's wrong. First, there are many things to rationally fear apart from fear itself. Second, we should not be afraid of fear—we should instead recognize it for what it is, and work to counteract it. In other words, we should observe its irrationality and refuse to be affected by it.

Rational fears can be quantified—you can see the spider, or the gun pointed at you, or your empty bank account. On the other hand, irrational fears are difficult, if not impossible, to quantify. Here's an example: when 152 people were infected with swine flu in Mexico in 2009, people around the world, prodded by the media's manufactured hysteria, erupted in fear of an epidemic. We were warned that the threat was everywhere—that everyone was potentially at risk; however, the data showed these fears to be completely unwarranted. Weeks into the "outbreak," there were around 1,000 reported cases of the virus in 20 countries. The number of fatalities stood at 26—25 in Mexico, and one in the United States (a boy who had just traveled to Texas from Mexico). Yet schools were closed, travel was restricted, emergency rooms were flooded, hundreds of thousands of pigs were killed, hand sanitizer and face masks disappeared from store shelves, and network news stories about swine flu consumed 43% of airtime.[9]

"There is too much hysteria in the country and so far, there hasn't been that great a danger," commented Congressman Ron Paul in response. "It's overblown, grossly so."[10] He should know. During Paul's first session in Congress in 1976, a swine flu outbreak led Congress to vote to vaccinate *the entire country*. (He voted against it.) Twenty-five people died from the vaccination itself, while only one person was killed from the actual virus; hundreds, if not more, contracted Guillain-Barre syndrome, a paralyzing neurological illness, as a result of the vaccine. Nearly 25 percent of the population was vaccinated before the effort was cancelled due to safety concerns.[11]

Again, the data did not substantiate the fear surrounding the swine flu. According to the Centers for Disease Control and Prevention, the seasonal flu infects 28 to 56 million Americans each year. Of those infected, some 100,000 are hospitalized and about 36,000 die. This means that, on average, around 150 deaths per day occur during the eight months of a normal flu season—every year. Stacking the swine flu numbers against these statistics shows how ill-founded our collective reaction was. But again, Americans were afraid of the unknown. They were paralyzed by the "nameless, unreasoning, unjustified terror" that an unseen threat induced. They were fearful of fear.

Remember Y2K? To save memory space on a computer, early programmers routinely wrote the year with only two numbers—1964 would be typed as 64, for example. Reaching the year 2000 would pose a problem for computers that couldn't distinguish between 1964 and 2064, and some programmers expressed concern that the dawn of the new century could cause computing chaos. Programs that depended on the date for critical decision making would behave oddly, it was warned, and even worse, some would simply stop.

The media was once again helpful in amplifying the threat and conjuring up all sorts of nightmare scenarios: downed airplanes, nuclear reactor meltdowns, emptied bank accounts, disconnected communication and power lines, unresponsive 911 dispatches, and empty grocery store shelves. The first minute on the first day of the first year in a new century came and went without incident. Hundreds of billions of dollars had been expended in remediation work— some of it admittedly necessary to upgrade computer systems—but no major incident occurred, and most now believe none would have.

Some fears are short-lived; when you take action to mitigate or avoid the circumstance that produced the emotion, it subsides. Other fears are prolonged and pervasive—paralyzing, even. While it's not possible for us to fully understand what life in a Middle Eastern country is like, let's listen to some of the people in their own words to see how constant this fear of fear has become.

"It's a continuous tension, a feeling of continuous uneasiness," said an American humanitarian worker in Pakistan. "We are scared. You wake up with a start to every noise."[12] A mother shares her perspective when members of her family hear a hovering drone overhead: "Because of the terror, we shut our eyes, hide under our scarves, put our hands over our ears."[13] A father of three children indicated, "Drones are always on my mind. It makes it difficult to sleep. They are like a mosquito. Even when you don't see them, you can hear them, you know they are there."[14] Another man stated, "I can't sleep at night because when the drones are there… I hear them making that sound, that noise. The drones are all over my brain, I can't sleep. When I hear the drones making that drone sound, I just turn on the light and sit there looking at the light. Whenever the drones are hovering over us, it just makes me so scared."[15] A local political leader added that people "often complain that they wake up in the middle of the night screaming because they are hallucinating about drones."[16] Think of the children. When they hear the drones, "They get really scared, and they can hear them all the time so they're always fearful that the drone is going to attack them,"[17] commented another individual. "Because of the noise, we're psychologically disturbed—women, men, and children. Twenty-four hours, a person is in stress and there is pain in his head."[18]

This constant state of fear was observed by a journalist who said that if you slam a door shut, Pakistani children will "scream and drop like something bad is going to happen."[19] People in this condition do not enjoy periods of peace, interspersed only rarely by threats. They face peril at any moment and have seen friends and family dismembered by a drone's bomb. Constantly afraid, what they most desire is relief—peace. Their tragedy helps us see how utterly incapacitating it can be to constantly be afraid of an unquantifiable, unidentifiable threat.

FEAR AS A WEAPON

Fear is not always unplanned and uninvited—sometimes it is deliberately manufactured. Because of its paralyzing potential, fear is often used as a tool of subjugation by those who seek to wield power over others. As the prolific author H.L. Mencken cynically said, "The whole aim of practical politics is to keep the populace alarmed (and hence clamorous to be led to safety) by menacing it with an endless series of hobgoblins, most of them imaginary."[20] When a threat is known and seen, the fight-or-flight response is beneficial. When the threat is not defined, there is nothing to fight or flee from. This creates a circumstance in which those who claim to be able to see the "hobgoblin" are given power and money in order to ostensibly fight it. Political leaders are apt to exaggerate or manufacture a threat so as to maximize their chance to accumulate power—to "do important things that you would otherwise avoid," in Rahm Emanuel's words.

As 9/11 is such an obvious example, let's continue with it. Since that fateful day, Americans have been scared incessantly by those in power, who have dominated the airwaves to repeatedly suggest the impending threat of more terrorism. If only they, our fearless leaders, could be trusted with more power (such as the USA PATRIOT Act), or given more money (trillions of taxpayer dollars having been spent on counterterrorism measures and foreign military interventions), or re-elected to continue their quest for freedom—if only we do *whatever they ask us to do*, then surely peace will be found around the corner.

Because the brain's response to fear is automatic, it can be exploited by those who wish to produce a desired effect. For example, a cruel boy who knows that his sister is easily scared of strange noises could torment her by playing random, scary sounds from his computer. Similarly, politicians know how best to frighten their constituents with hobgoblins, producing a consistent response—usually in the form of support for whatever policy is proposed to keep us safe. This exploitation is done with an end in mind: the tormenting brother might consider his cruelty a form of entertainment and pleasure; politicians might simply desire a given policy for which public support is lacking, or they might like to receive large campaign donations from influential corporations with heavy ties to what President Dwight D. Eisenhower called the "military industrial complex."[21]

In the aftermath of 9/11, Republicans gained control of both chambers of Congress heading into the 2004 campaign season. Guest speakers and candidates lined up at the Republican National Convention, each referencing and emphasizing the events of 9/11, the need to fight terrorism, the menace of Saddam Hussein, and related threats. They discussed, repeatedly, the "hour of danger," the "very dangerous world," a "grave, new threat," the terrorists' "horrific acts of atrocities," people "dedicated to killing us," torture chambers, mass graves, radical ideologies, deadly technologies, and of course, "weapons of mass destruction."[22] Fear was, as journalist Glenn Greenwald once wrote, the "one very potent weapon" that the Bush administration had in its arsenal, which it repeatedly used. He continued:

> Ever since September 11, 2001, Americans have been
> bombarded with warnings, with color-coded "alerts,"

with talk of mushroom clouds and nefarious plots to blow up bridges and tall buildings, with villains assigned cartoon names such as "dirty bomber," "Dr. Germ," and so on. And there has been a constant barrage from the White House of impending threats that generate fear—fear of terrorism, fear of more 9/11–style attacks, fear of nuclear annihilation, fear of our ports being attacked, fear of our water systems being poisoned—and, of course, fear of excessive civil liberties or cumbersome laws jeopardizing our "homeland security."

Our very survival is at risk, we are told. We face an enemy unlike any we have seen before, more powerful than anything we have previously encountered. President Bush is devoted to protecting us from the terrorists. We have to invade and occupy Iraq because the terrorists will kill us all if we do not. We must allow the president to incarcerate American citizens without due process, employ torture as a state-sanctioned weapon, eavesdrop on our private conversations, and even violate the law, because the terrorists are so evil and so dangerous that we cannot have any limits on the power of the president if we want him to protect us from the dangers in the world.[23]

The same talking points were repeated for years afterward. When the news of the Bush administration's eavesdropping program broke in early 2006, Vice President Dick Cheney was summoned, among other supporters, to defend the clearly illegal program on grounds that it was necessary to protect the country. "As we get farther away from September 11th," Cheney said, "some in Washington are yielding to the temptation to downplay the ongoing threat to our country, and to back away from the business at hand…. The enemy that struck on 9/11 is weakened and fractured, yet it is still lethal and trying to hit us again. Either we are serious about fighting this war or we are not."

You'll note, of course, that he did not respond to the criticisms against the eavesdropping program, nor did he provide any rational basis for its use. All he did was play on the fears of Americans to justify the violation of the law. As support for the Middle Eastern military interventions began to subside years later, the key architects continued their fearmongering. In June 2014, Cheney stepped forward to speak out about the continued threat in Iraq and warned—despite having been proven wrong about key foreign policy claims in the past—that there would be an attack on the United States within the next decade that would be even worse than those on 9/11. "I think there will be another attack," he said. "And the next time, I think it's going to be far deadlier than the last one. Imagine what would happen if somebody could smuggle a nuclear device, put it in a shipping container, and drive it down the beltway outside Washington, D.C."[24]

"Neither a man nor a crowd nor a nation can be trusted to act humanely or to think sanely under the influence of a great fear," wrote the British philosopher Bertrand Russell.[25] Thus we see individuals condoning torture, deprivation, incarceration, and even murder under the pretense that doing so will abate their fears and help them feel safe. We similarly see the populace complying with insane demands to submit to molestation at the airport as a necessary measure for ensuring their protection. There is almost no end to what people will do in hopes of being kept safe from the supposed hobgoblins that threaten them. As Benjamin Franklin observed, most will go so far as to alienate their birthright of liberty—and those who do "deserve neither liberty nor safety."[26]

Though problematic, it's easy to see why people are so ready to surrender their freedom in pursuit of safety. After all, if civilization itself were on the very verge of destruction as is so often suggested, few people would get upset over a few legal bumps in the road. Consider how many people enjoy watching the television show "24"—because viewers see and understand the threat, they don't object much to parts of the plot that show torture, eavesdropping, kidnapping, and related criminality. If Jack Bauer is saving millions of lives, what's the fuss if he ends a few along the way? Viewers don't hate Jack for doing it—they shower him with praise and adoration. He's a savior.

This ends-justifies-the-means stratagem is likewise employed by politicians who claim that their actions, however legally dubious they may be, are necessary to keep Americans safe. The more skeptical among us might see these actions as a means for simply enriching or empowering the politicians. Some consider it radical—preposterous, even—to suggest that political leaders would purposefully engage in activities and implement policies designed to create a state of fear, but plenty of scholarship backs up this assertion.[27] And, of course, we're generally comfortable with the idea that foreign governments employ this tactic against people in other countries. Known as "psychological warfare" (PSYWAR), the intentional creation and exploitation of fear is a method of war in which the attack is not on the infrastructure of another country or the bodies of its soldiers, but rather their psyche. This type of attack is much less effective if the individual becomes aware that his psyche is being manipulated, so secrecy is crucial, and the target must be kept in the dark.

Weapons are most often used in wartime, of course, so it's not surprising to see weaponized fear implemented in the context of armed hostilities. In other words, fear of inflation or global warming has a lesser effect than does a fear of bodily harm or death. People are less disposed to react with fear towards a delayed threat—as Thomas Jefferson said, "mankind are more disposed to suffer" than to proactively improve their circumstances. But when government officials use alarming terms and shocking hypotheticals to alert us to the dangers inherent in the *terror du jour*, the fear is almost palpable. Throughout history, war has been a desirable tool for authoritarians. It is, in Randolph Bourne's words, the "health of the state."[28] But the average citizen is unwilling to die in combat for unjust reasons; we don't look kindly upon waging war in order to secure access to oil in a foreign country, or to depose a ruler that is an obstacle to the interests of global corporations. "Why, of course, the *people* don't want war," observed Hermann Göring, one of the highest ranking Nazis, who survived the war to be captured and put on trial for war crimes. He continued:

> Why would some poor slob on a farm want to risk his life in a war when the best that he can get out of it is to come back to his farm in one piece? Naturally, the common people don't want war; neither in Russia nor in England nor in America, nor for that matter in Germany. That is understood. But, after all, it is the *leaders* of the country who determine the policy and it is always a simple matter to drag the people along, whether it is a democracy or a fascist dictatorship or a Parliament or a Communist dictatorship.[29]

"There is one difference," pointed out Göring's interviewer. "In a democracy the people have some say in the matter through their elected representatives, and in the United States only Congress can declare wars." This was quickly dismissed by Göring: "Oh, that is all well and good, but, voice or no voice, the people can always be brought to the bidding of the leaders. That is easy. All you have to do is tell them they are being attacked and denounce the pacifists for lack of patriotism and exposing the country to danger. It works the same way in any country."

Another reason politicians use fear as a weapon, primarily in the context of war, is for personal gain, power, and prestige. Robert Higgs, senior fellow in political economy at the Independent Institute, explains:

> Even absolute monarchs can get bored. The exercise of great power may become tedious and burdensome— underlings are always disturbing your serenity with questions about details; victims are always appealing for clemency, pardons, or exemptions from your rules. In

wartime, however, rulers come alive. Nothing equals war as an opportunity for greatness and public acclaim, as all such leaders understand. Condemned to spend their time in high office during peacetime, they are necessarily condemned to go down in history as mediocrities at best.

Upon the outbreak of war, however, the exhilaration of the hour spreads through the entire governing apparatus. Army officers who had languished for years at the rank of captain may now anticipate becoming colonels. Bureau heads who had supervised a hundred subordinates with a budget of $1 million may look forward to overseeing a thousand with a budget of $20 million. Powerful new control agencies must be created and staffed. New facilities must be built, furnished, and operated. Politicians who had found themselves frozen in partisan gridlock can now expect that the torrent of money gushing from the public treasury will grease the wheels for putting together humongous legislative deals undreamt of in the past. Everywhere the government turns its gaze, the scene is flush with energy, power, and money. For those whose hands direct the machinery of a government at war, life has never been better.[30]

A weapon can be used on anybody, and makes no distinction between friend or foe. A firearm, for example, can be used both offensively and defensively. It can be used to shoot an intruder, innocent individual, or oneself. Similarly, fear can be used on external enemies, but it can also be used inwardly on one's own countrymen and colleagues. Senate Majority Leader Harry Reid, a Democrat, invoked the fear of chaos by referring to his Republican colleagues as "anarchists," and House Minority Leader Nancy Pelosi, also a Democrat, called House Republicans "legislative arsonists." Echoing her colleagues, Condoleezza Rice began grooming Americans for war in Iraq in 2003 by ominously warning, "There will always be some uncertainty about how quickly [they] can acquire nuclear weapons. But we don't want the smoking gun to be a mushroom cloud."[31] President Bush took to the airwaves to argue, "What this government has done is to take steps necessary to protect you and your family… We're at war. This is people that want to come and kill your families… This isn't make-believe."[32] Amid a sense of heightened panic surrounding a sluggish economy, the same president took steps to intervene, including authorizing taxpayer-funded bailouts for failing corporations, arguing that he "abandoned free market principles to save the free market system."[33] Creating plumes of thick smoke persuades people to believe that there's a large fire that needs extinguishing; when the smoke clears and people see the previous threat for what it was (or, rather, for what it *wasn't*), only then do they realize they've been duped. But it's usually too late to reverse course—the power has been centralized, the money has been spent, and the key players have gotten off the hook. As Ronald Reagan said, the permanency of the programs put in place by government are the "nearest thing to eternal life we'll ever see on this earth."

FEAR AS A CHOICE

We're all familiar with the fable about the boy who cried wolf. A shepherd boy repeatedly tricked nearby villagers into thinking that a wolf was attacking his flock of sheep. After multiple "false alarms," the wolf actually did attack. But this time, when the boy called for help as he had many times before, the villagers did not respond. Reality is also filled with false alarms ("hobgoblins," as Mencken said) and fearmongering authority figures who sound the same cry, time and again. Will we continue to listen to them?

As the federal government's military interventions spread to Afghanistan, Pakistan, and elsewhere, Iraq fell into the shadows of public consciousness for several years. But in early 2014, a sectarian Sunni militia known as the Islamic State in Iraq and Syria (ISIS) began to push back against a small, ineffective Iraqi military, gaining control of several cities. Their quick gains and gruesome tactics thrust Iraq back into the spotlight, with many politicians and pundits arguing that further intervention was needed to stabilize the region and protect America's "interests." Fear, once again, was their weapon of choice; Americans were presented with one doomsday scenario after another.

But Iraq was not a fresh landscape for American foreign policy. Here's the rundown after a decade of American military intervention: over 4,400 U.S. military deaths and tens of thousands of soldiers disfigured and otherwise wounded; somewhere between 150,000 and 1,500,000 Iraqi civilians killed;[34] over three trillion taxpayer dollars spent in direct and indirect costs; and more than a million soldiers deployed. Of course, this doesn't include U.S. military interventions in other countries, nor does it address the often underreported results of prolonged warfare, such as rampant divorce,[35] alarmingly frequent sexual abuse,[36] and high levels of suicide among soldiers,[37] etc.

With this data as a backdrop, consider the conversations presented to the American public, couched in terms of fear. News stations packed their lineups with the very same people who had been crying wolf for a decade—architects of the entire war in Iraq, such as Dick Cheney, Condoleezza Rice, Paul Wolfowitz, Bill Kristol, and others. These were the individuals who, along with their fearmongering, assuaged the consciences of Americans by claiming that U.S. forces would be greeted as liberators and that the war would be financed through oil revenue. These were the ones falsely claiming that Saddam Hussein had weapons of mass destruction, which, if left unchecked by "shock and awe" style military campaigns, would jeopardize American interests.

And these were the ones invited to once again warn the villagers of an impending wolf, despite their clearly compromised track record.

For example, as ISIS began targeting and terminating Iraq's Christian minority population, these interventionists and their ideological allies throughout the media began calling for intervention—not revealing to the public, of course, that these Christians had been protected under Saddam Hussein, whose administration they first destabilized and ultimately destroyed. While the architects of war in Iraq were given dozens of interviews, those who originally opposed the war in Iraq after 9/11 were often left out of the conversation altogether. Consider former congressman Kent Conrad, who was one of only 23 to vote against authorizing the use of force in Iraq. When asked whether he had ever been interviewed about the new proposals to intervene in Iraq, he replied, simply, "Not once."[38] A well-known journalist who was critical of the justifications used to lead the nation into war, Jonathan Landay, was likewise sidelined and opined that the media consistently gives the fearmongers a platform "to create controversy, and that controversy will be enhanced by whatever they say, irrespective of whether it's accurate or not."[39] Landay also offered the following observation:

> The analogy I'd draw is the following: You go to a doctor, who diagnoses an ailment and prescribes drugs and surgery. The diagnosis, however, turns out to be disastrously wrong and as a result, the drugs and surgery leave you crippled for years to come. Are you going to go back to that same doctor to diagnose your next illness? No, you aren't. In fact, you probably sued him/her for malpractice after the first go-round. Unfortunately, we can't sue Bush, Cheney, Rumsfeld, Wolfowitz, Rice, Feith and the others for malpractice. But we can stop listening to them.

He's exactly right: we can stop listening. This is our choice, and our opportunity. Fear is only a potent weapon *because we allow it to be.* Like the villagers in the fable, we can stop listening to those who cry wolf. We are the ones who give them their power. Recall that Göring said that people can "always" be brought to do the bidding of their leaders through the use of fear, and historically that's generally been true—rarely are many people sufficiently skeptical to shut down the attempts of political leaders who lie their way into more power and policy changes. But every time it happens—every time they cry wolf—we have a choice. We can listen and support their proposed remedies, or we can choose not to listen to them and instead actively oppose them. Imagine if the villagers got so fed up with the young shepherd that they funded the creation of a tower to oversee the nearby area and paid for a person they trusted to keep watch. The shepherd would be out of business, unable to deceive them anymore.

The reason fear is such an effective political weapon is that individuals do not have the facts necessary to make an informed decision. When Americans were told by the President of the United States that Saddam Hussein possessed and was planning to use weapons of mass destruction, how could they know otherwise? Most people couldn't finance a trip to Iraq to verify for themselves, and those who could would not have the connections, resources, or knowledge to complete the task.

We naturally defer the decision making to those who have access to greater political and military intelligence than the general population. Christopher Guzelian, a legal theorist, posits that politicians are so successful in their use of fear because of "risk information (whether correct or false) that is communicated to society." In other words, we fear the hobgoblin we can't see solely on the basis that we're told he exists and is coming after us. Guzelian concludes that it is "risk communication, not personal experience, [that] causes most fear these days."[40]

This is a point that cannot be stressed enough. Wolves are rarely seen on an individual basis by villagers; we rely upon trusted sources to communicate to us the risks we need to be aware of (and, in turn, afraid of). As a result, writes one author, "Fear is decreasingly experienced first-hand and increasingly experienced on a discursive and abstract level."[41] We can't see the danger, we lack information, and we line up in support of whatever policy is considered necessary to keep us feeling safe and happy.

Wilton Sekzer is a former NYPD cop and father of two. One of his sons, Jason, died on 9/11 when one of the planes hit the tower in which he worked. Sekzer was furious, and wanted revenge. "Somebody had to pay for 9/11," he said, recounting his feelings years later. "I want the enemy dead. I want to see their bodies stacked up for what they did—for taking my son."[42] He persistently and successfully lobbied the military to write his son's name on a bomb. "In loving memory of Jason Sekzer" was painted on a 2,000-pound, laser-guided bomb before it shortly thereafter "met with 100% success" according to the soldier who sent Sezker photos showing that his request had been fulfilled. But a few weeks later, his anger turned from the Middle Eastern terrorists to the Oval Office.

After 9/11, the Bush administration chose Saddam Hussein as its hobgoblin and began using suggestion and innuendo to direct Americans' anger toward Iraq. No outright claim was made that the regime was responsible for the 9/11 attacks, but carefully crafted statements in which "9/11" and "Iraq" were frequently mentioned together led much of the public to believe that it was. Certainly no effort was made to correct the assumption. Months into the war, a reporter backed the president into a corner on the issue, leading him to reply that "we've had no evidence that Saddam Hussein was involved" with the 9/11 attacks.[43]

"I almost jumped out of the chair," said Sezker. "What is he nuts, or what? What the hell did we go in there for?" Even a week after the president admitted that there was no connection between Iraq and 9/11, a poll showed that 69 percent of Americans still believed that Hussein was personally involved. They, like Sekzer, had been duped. "I was mad," Sekzer recalled. He continued:

> My first thought is: you're a liar. I'm from the old school. Certain people walk on water, and the President

of the United States is one of them. If I can't trust the President of the United States, I don't know… it's a terrible thing when American citizens can't trust their president. You begin to wonder, what the hell is with the whole system? There's something wrong with the entire system! The government exploited my feelings of patriotism, of a deep desire for revenge for what happened to my son. But I was so insane with wanting to "get even," I was willing to believe anything.[44]

Sekzer's emotional response led him to accept as fact what he was told by political leaders without questioning their integrity or motives. He thought the war in Iraq was justified, and that placing his son's name on a 2,000-pound bomb, as an implement of war to kill untold numbers of Iraqis on the ground below, would honor his son's memory. Sekzer wasn't alone, of course; the government exploited the feelings of patriotism and revenge—using fear as a weapon—of hundreds of millions of people. Almost none of these people had experienced the events of 9/11 directly, nor did they have direct knowledge of the purported threats about weapons of mass destruction. Lacking this, they based their fear on the "risk communication" being delivered to them—the fearmongering that pervaded all forms of media in the weeks, months, and even years following the attacks.

You and I don't have access to the same intelligence that the government has, but we can still make informed decisions. Just as the villagers noticed a pattern and learned to ignore the shepherd, we can look for patterns of abuse of power, conflicts of interest, and track records of public deception. This becomes extremely useful information, just as it was for the villagers—and though we lack information to corroborate or refute the claims being made about a wolf sighting, we at least have an idea about the trustworthiness of the shepherd. In a global survey conducted in late 2013, only 44% of university-educated people worldwide indicated that they trust their government.[45] In the United States during the same year, the trust level continued its downward trend, likely due to Edward Snowden's revelations about illegal eavesdropping activity by the NSA and the recent government shutdown fiasco; in 2013, 50% of poll respondents said they trust the federal government "not very much" or "not at all."[46] As can be seen in the chart below (which shows the level of trust in government according to polls conducted by Gallup), trust levels have changed over time, peaking after 9/11. Gallup notes that "In the aftermath of the Sept. 11 terrorist attacks, Americans 'rallied' around their government and leaders, expressing unusually high levels of trust and confidence in their ability to deal with the country's problems."[47]

How much of the time do you think you can trust government in Washington to do what is right — just about always, most of the time, or only some of the time?

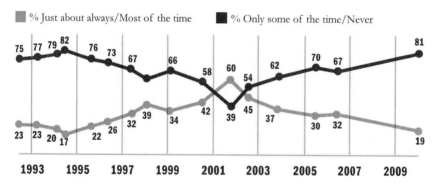

Source: "Trust in Government," Gallup, http://www.gallup.com/poll/5392/trust-government.aspx

When an actual attack occurred on 9/11, and politicians began menacing Americans with an "endless series of hobgoblins" in the form of weapons of mass destruction and other purported threats, confidence in government climbed—just as Göring explained. Politicians and pundits often worry about distrust in the government, scrambling for explanations and solutions. But a healthy amount of skepticism is a good thing, for as Voltaire said, "Those who can make you believe absurdities, can make you commit atrocities."[48] If Americans hadn't believed the absurdities they were told about Saddam Hussein, they likely would not have supported the atrocity of killing hundreds of thousands of Iraqis as part of a "shock and awe" offensive war campaign.

The Matrix is a fascinating science fiction film depicting a dystopian future in which humans live within a simulated reality. One of its best scenes comes near the end, when the lead character, Neo, is shot by an "agent"—the controlling antagonist whose mission it is to exterminate those who have broken free from the system. Seemingly dead for some time, Neo then rises from the ground, suddenly aware of the power he now has—he, and not the agents, controls the system. In frustration, several agents fire their weapons at Neo, but the dozens of bullets stop mid-air at his command. He curiously reaches for one bullet, inspects it, and then lets it drop to the ground. The others likewise drop. Apart from this exercise of his newfound power, what's interesting—almost humorous—is the expressions on the faces of the agents. They're astonished, even dumbfounded, that Neo didn't die, and worse still, that he was successfully fighting back.

Like Neo within the Matrix, we live under a controlling government that prefers we remain asleep within the system, believing the false narrative we're constantly fed. Fear is its weapon, used without restraint in psychological warfare. We, sadly and shockingly, are the enemy—and we will continue to be defeated until we learn, like Neo, how to take control. It begins with a choice. We must be purposefully skeptical of supposed shepherds who repeatedly deceive us, whatever their motives may be. We must choose to seek out reputable sources of information with established records of accuracy and integrity. Even then, as Ronald Reagan often said, we should "Trust, but verify." We must choose to constantly be suspicious that our fears may be triggered not through personal experience and verifiable evidence, but through claims made to us regarding dangers we cannot see. As the saying goes, "Fool me once, shame on you; fool me twice, shame on me."

NOTES

1. Henry David Thoreau, *Excursions* (Arc Manor, 2008), 22.

2. Daniel Goleman, *Emotional Intelligence: Why It Can Matter More Than IQ* (New York: Bantam Books, 2005), 17.

3. Antonio Damasio, *Descartes' Error* (New York: Avon Books, 1994), 8.

4. "Who's afraid to fly on September 11? ," CNN, September 11, 2012, accessed August 2, 2014, http://www.cnn.com/2012/09/11/travel/fear-travel-september-11/.

5. "Despite recent accidents, airplane travel still safest," MSN News, July 26, 2013, accessed August 2, 2014, http://news.msn.com/us/despite-recent-accidents-airplane-travel-still-safest.

6. "Congress Had No Time to Read the USA PATRIOT Act," Sunlight Foundation, accessed August 2, 2014, http://sunlightfoundation.com/blog/2009/03/02/congress-had-no-time-to-read-the-usa-patriot-act/.

7. "President Establishes Office of Homeland Security," Summary of the President's Executive Order, October 8, 2001, accessed August 2, 2014, http://www.dhs.gov/xnews/releases/press_release_0010.shtm.

8. Davis W. Houck, *FDR and Fear Itself: The First Inaugural Address* (Texas A&M University Press, 2002), 3.

9. "Did We Overreact To Swine Flu Threat?," CBS News, May 6, 2009, accessed August 2, 2014, http://www.cbsnews.com/news/did-we-overreact-to-swine-flu-threat/.

10. "Hysteria over swine flu is the real danger, some say," CNN, May 4, 2009, accessed August 2, 2014, http://www.cnn.com/2009/HEALTH/05/03/swine.flu.react/.

11. "Swine flu 'debacle' of 1976 is recalled," *USA Today*, April 27, 2009, accessed August 2, 2014, http://articles.latimes.com/2009/apr/27/science/sci-swine-history27.

12. "'Every Person Is Afraid of the Drones': The Strikes' Effect on Life in Pakistan," The Atlantic, September 25, 2012, accessed August 2,

2014, http://www.theatlantic.com/international/archive/2012/09/ every-person-is-afraid-of-the-drones-the-strikes-effect-on-life-in-pakistan/262814/.

13. Ibid.

14. Ibid.

15. Ibid.

16. Ibid.

17. Ibid.

18. Ibid.

19. Ibid.

20. H.L. Mencken, *In Defense of Women* (1918).

21. Suzanne McIntire, *Speeches in World History* (New York: Facts on File, Inc., 2009), 445.

22. "Bush Republican Fear-Mongering," YouTube, accessed August 2, 2014, https://www.youtube.com/watch?v=83XcGFIBmxY.

23. "Fear as a Weapon," Mother Jones, July 7, 2006, accessed August 2, 2014, http://www.motherjones.com/politics/2006/07/fear-weapon.

24. "Dick Cheney: There will be an attack on America within the next decade; worse than 9/11," YouTube, accessed August 2, 2014, https://www.youtube.com/watch?v=qrD7N2JMaJc.

25. Bertrand Russell, *Unpopular Essays* (New York: Routledge, 1995), 121.

26. Benjamin Franklin, *The Memoirs of Benjamin Franklin, vol. 2* (Philadelphia: McCarty & Davis, 1834), 99. The full quote reads: "Those who would give up essential Liberty, to purchase a little temporary Safety, deserve neither Liberty nor Safety."

27. See: Ted Brader, "Striking a Responsive Chord: How Political Ads Motivate and Persuade Voters by Appealing to Emotions," *American Journal of Political Science* 49(2): 388-405; Paul R. Abramson, John H. Aldrich, Jill Rickerhauser, and David W. Rohde, "Fear in the Voting Booth: The 2004 Presidential Election," *Political Behavior* 29(2):197-220; and Peter K. Hatemi, "Fear as a disposition and an emotional state: A genetic and environmental approach to political preferences," *American Journal of Political Science* 57(2): 279–293.

28. Bruce Clayton, *Forgotten Prophet: The Life of Randolph Bourne* (University of Missouri, 1998), 252.

29. G.M. Gilbert, *Nuremberg Diary* (Cambridge: Da Capo Press, Inc., 1995), 278.

30. Robert Higgs, "Fear: The Foundation of Every Government's Power," Independent Institute, May 17, 2005, accessed August 2, 2014.

31. "Search for the 'smoking gun'," CNN, January 10, 2003, accessed August 2, 2014, http://www.cnn.com/2003/US/01/10/wbr.smoking.gun/.

32. "FearWatch: The Fear-Mongering Hall of Shame," *The Huffington Post*, September 18, 2006, accessed August 2, 2014, http://www.huffingtonpost.com/arianna-huffington/fearwatch-the-fearmongeri_b_29737.html.

33. "State of the Union with Candy Crowley," CNN, November 14, 2010, accessed August 2, 2014, http://transcripts.cnn.com/TRANSCRIPTS/1011/14/sotu.02.html.

34. Because of incomplete data, the estimates vary and are highly contested.

35. "Military Divorce Risk Increases With Lengthy Deployments," *The Huffington Post*, September 3, 2013, accessed August 2, 2014.

36. One in three military women has been sexually assaulted, compared to one in six civilian women. See "Military Sexual Assault Epidemic Continues To Claim Victims As Defense Department Fails Females," *The Huffington Post*, May 20, 2013, accessed August 2, 2014.

37. One soldier commits suicide every two to three days. See "War-years military suicide rate higher than believed," *USA Today*, April 25, 2014, accessed August 2, 2014, http://www.usatoday.com/story/nation/2014/04/25/suicide-rates-army-military-pentagon/8060059/

38. "If You Were An Iraq War Critic, You're Probably Not Being Asked To Go On TV," *The Huffington Post*, June 27, 2014, accessed August 2, 2014.

39. Ibid.

40. Christopher Guzelian, "Liability and Fear" (Stanford Public Law and Legal Theory Working Paper Series: Stanford, 2004.), 712, 767.

41. Stefanie Grupp, "Political Implications Of A Discourse Of Fear; The Mass Mediated Discourse Of Fear In the Aftermath Of 9/11," (Unpublished paper: Berlin, 2003), 43.

42. *Why We Fight*, directed by Eugene Jarecki (2005).

43. "Bush: No Saddam Links To 9/11," CBS News, November 18, 2003, accessed August 2, 2014.

44. Ibid.

45. "Distrust in government growing, survey finds," *USA Today*, January 20, 2014, accessed August 2, 2014, http://www.usatoday.com/story/news/world/2014/01/20/distrust-in-government-growing/4655111/.

46. "Trust in Government," Gallup, accessed August 2, 2014, http://www.gallup.com/poll/5392/trust-government.aspx.

47. "Trust in Government Falls to Pre-9/11 Levels," Gallup, October 6, 2003, accessed August 2, 2014, http://www.gallup.com/poll/9394/trust-government-falls-pre911-levels.aspx.

48. Voltaire, *Oeuvres complètes de Voltaire, vol. 1* (Paris: Aug. Ozanne, 1838), 96.

FEAR AND IGNORANCE

*"Power-lust is a weed that grows only in the
vacant lots of an abandoned mind."*[1]
—Ayn Rand

FULGENCIO BATISTA WAS THE ELECTED president of Cuba from 1940 to 1944. He then moved to the United States of America, returning to Cuba to run for president once more in 1952. Facing electoral defeat, Batista led a military coup and took control of the government. He subsequently suspended the Constitution, censored the media, banned a whole host of activities, and used police forces to torture and publicly execute thousands of individuals. For several years he benefited from financial, military, and logistical support provided by the United States government. His dictatorial reign ended in 1959, when Fidel Castro, a 32-year-old lawyer, led a rebel army to violently overthrow Batista's regime, making Cuba the first communist state in the Western Hemisphere.

Castro began nationalizing large businesses in order to centralize economic control, while establishing close ties with the Soviet Union. The United States of America, for its part, broke off diplomatic relations. In March 1960, President Dwight D. Eisenhower authorized the CIA to organize, train, and equip over 1,400 Cuban refugees as a paramilitary force to overthrow Castro. Their attempt, the following year, was unsuccessful. The "Bay of Pigs" incident, as it's known, was over within three days, and the CIA-backed forces surrendered, were interrogated, and were sent back to the United States of America. As tensions further escalated, the federal government organized the "Cuban Project" (also known as Operation Mongoose) which entailed political, military, and psychological attacks, including assassination attempts on leaders within the Castro regime.

Part of this project was Operation Northwoods, a series of proposals calling for the CIA to commit acts of terrorism within the United States to be blamed on Cuba. "The desired resultant from the execution of this plan," the proposal read, "would be to place the United States in the apparent position of suffering defensible grievances from a rash and irresponsible government of Cuba and to develop an international image of a Cuban threat to peace in the Western Hemisphere." It recommended creating a "Communist Cuban terror campaign in the Miami area, in other Florida cities and even in Washington"—a campaign which included hijacking airplanes, blowing up a U.S. ship in Guantanamo Bay, bombing American cities, and sinking boatloads of Cuban refugees desperately seeking a better life. All of this was proposed because "it would seem desirable to use legitimate provocation as the basis for U.S. military intervention in Cuba"; therefore a "cover and deception plan" was seen as beneficial. In other words, government officials wanted to create public support for aggressive and unprovoked military interventions in Cuba but knew that it likely wouldn't happen without a hobgoblin to scare Americans into supporting their plan.

Operation Northwoods was not created by some crackpot academic or revolutionary radical. This proposal to perform terrorist acts within the country and blame them on Cuba, all for political gain, was drafted and approved by the Joint Chiefs of Staff—a group of senior military officials within the United States Department of Defense. It was ultimately and personally rejected by President John F. Kennedy.

This type of proposal is called a "false flag" and has been used many times throughout history. As we saw in the last chapter, physical attacks lead to a corresponding increase of trust in political leaders and submission to them. This effect is likely the same whether the attack be a surprise, known to political leaders yet allowed to happen, or directly orchestrated by these same leaders who stand to benefit from the increased trust and submission, as was the case in Operation Northwoods. False flag operations are used because people generally do not have access to the details, so they are prone to rely upon what they're told, and thus are easily deceived. People will, for the most part, believe what they are told in times of crisis, and so government officials, whether their motives are good or evil, capitalize on or completely fabricate the crises.

The world was shocked in 1990 as a young Kuwaiti woman identified only by her first name, Nayirah, testified through tears before the Congressional Human Rights Caucus regarding crimes committed by Iraqi soldiers. Nayirah claimed that soldiers took babies out of incubators in a Kuwaiti hospital and left them to die. Representative John Porter, co-chairman of the caucus, afterward stated that in his eight years of service he had never heard such "brutality and inhumanity and sadism."[2] Many senators cited Nayirah's testimony in their speeches supporting military intervention against Iraq, and President George Bush repeated the story several times in the following weeks. News media widely publicized portions of her testimony. To say that Americans were shocked and outraged would be an understatement—the allegations made in the testimony were, after all, quite alarming.

They were also false.

Only later was it discovered that Nayirah was the daughter of the Kuwaiti ambassador to the United States, and that she had been coached by an advertising agency that was paid millions of dollars by Citizens for a Free Kuwait—a public relations committee created by officials at the Kuwaiti embassy. As one reporter wrote, "The incubator story seriously distorted the American debate about whether to support military action."[3] But that was the point; Hill & Knowlton, the advertising agency coaching Nayirah and others, had spent a million dollars provided by the Kuwaiti royal family to determine how best to sway American public opinion.[4] Robin Andersen, author of *A Century of Media, A Century of War*, explains:

> Polls commissioned by Hill & Knowlton from the Republican political consulting firm The Wirthlin Group showed a lack of support for intervention. Wirthlin conducted focus groups to determine a strategy that could change public opinion. They found that atrocity stories stirred anger and encouraged sentiments in favor of war. The babies-thrown-out-of-their-incubators tale was particularly effective.[5]

Interestingly, but perhaps unsurprisingly, the agency's Washington office was headed up by President Bush's former chief of staff, Craig Fuller. After the truth came out, a corroborating witness—a doctor who had presented himself as a surgeon, but was actually a dentist—retracted most of his testimony. Additionally, he, along with other witnesses, used a false name. None of this was known to the gullible public that bought their story and chose to support military intervention. Lacking data to assess the nature and legitimacy of the threat, they trusted the communicated risk and once again supported policies they might have otherwise opposed.

Just two days before the ceasefire, American and Canadian forces attacked retreating Iraqi military personnel and others escaping Kuwait. The destruction of hundreds of vehicles along with their occupants became known as the "Highway of Death" and the images produced from the resulting carnage became some of the most recognizable of the war. Kenneth Jarecke's photo never attained widespread recognition, though it might have. Jarecke was a photojournalist covering the Gulf War who snapped a scene along the Highway of Death of the charred remains of an Iraqi soldier, his last grimace of pain frozen on his melted face as he tried to get out of his burning car. Prior to taking the photo, Jarecke wrote in chalk on the truck, "If I don't photograph this, people like my mom will think war is what they see on TV." The photo was censored; just as fear-inducing false flags sway public opinion in support of war, photos such as Jarecke's can shift it in the opposite direction. This is why President George Bush, just before the start of the Gulf War, banned journalists from taking photos of the flag-draped coffins of deceased soldiers returning home from war. Nevertheless, though Jarecke's image was not widely circulated, other photos of the Highway of Death affected public opinion and were cited as a factor in President Bush's decision to end hostilities. Colin Powell, then Chairman of the Joint Chiefs of Staff, expressed concern that the photos, coupled with the resulting television coverage, were "starting to make it look as if we were engaged in slaughter for slaughter's sake."[6]

THE RISK OF IGNORANCE

The point not to be missed here is that information—or the lack thereof—shapes public opinion. More specifically, a person's beliefs and decisions are affected by the information at his disposal. If a person's understanding is limited only to sound bites conveyed by politicians and pundits—risk communication—then he will most likely believe what he is told. On the other hand, if this person sees photos or video of the carnage—if he realizes that innocent people are suffering, or that the force being used is disproportionate and offensive—then there is a chance that he will object to the hostilities. As more people share information about what is actually going on, contextualizing and checking the claims being made by government officials, public support shifts accordingly. This isn't rocket science— yet time and again, people form beliefs and make decisions in the absence of any real evidence. As Shakespeare once wrote, "folly and ignorance" are the "common curse of mankind."[7]

Aldous Huxley, a writer best known for his dystopian novel *Brave New World*, once wrote that "The greatest triumphs of propaganda have been accomplished not by doing something, but by refraining from doing. Great is truth, but still greater, from a practical point of view, is silence about truth."[8] Ignorance, then, is fear's greatest catalyst; predatory politicians prefer a blindfolded people who can neither see nor respond to what's actually around them.

Think of the Central Intelligence Agency whose agents operate in the shadows dethroning foreign leaders, training and arming guerrilla forces, torturing people, and engaging in other subversive activities. Would Americans support and fund their operations if they were known? Or think of the National Security Agency. Their operations, which include mass surveillance and bulk data collection of innocent people not suspected of any crimes, were based upon a prevalent fear that somebody, somewhere, might be plotting an attack. Their success was contingent upon the ignorance of their targets.

In June 2013 when Edward Snowden leaked a trove of confidential documents outlining the agency's activities, people all around the world went from ignorant to informed. They then changed their beliefs and opinions; polls conducted in the months following showed a significant spike in the number of people concerned about and opposed to the NSA's activities, as well as increased support for transparency, oversight, and reform.[9]

When challenged over the years, especially since 9/11, lawyers for the government have routinely hidden these types of activities behind a claim of "national security privilege," arguing that the disclosure of the requested or relevant information would compromise "national security." But President Obama, forced into a corner by the opposition resulting from the leaks, subsequently ordered the Director of National Intelligence to produce a "transparency report" on one of the most un-transparent government entities. A year after Snowden's leaks, the first-of-its-kind report was issued.[10] This report, let alone the passionate and productive debate on civil liberties and privacy, would never have happened without the data provided by Snowden— which the government was unwilling to furnish voluntarily.

Plato once said that "ignorance is the root of misfortune," but he didn't go far enough. It's not that misfortune happens to befall the ignorant, by mere happenstance. Rather, as we remain ignorant or naïve, we expose ourselves to the rapacious plots of scheming individuals looking to get away with something—sometimes through overt acts of fear-based propaganda, but more often, as Huxley said, through "silence about truth." Further, a person's ignorance necessarily puts him into a state of submission to these power-brokers, allowing them to continue their charade of hobgoblins and fearmongering. All of this combined allows fear to be widely and frequently used as a weapon to further the interests of those who stand to benefit. Rightly did Thomas Jefferson say, "If a nation expects to be ignorant and free, in a state of civilization, it expects what never was and never will be."[11]

Today we are told, either explicitly or in various roundabout ways, that we should be afraid of another terrorist attack. We are informed that the government has prevented more of them from happening— but no, we can't have any details about these claims that would verify (or debunk) them. We are encouraged to support ongoing and increasing interventions in the Middle East and elsewhere, ostensibly to neutralize future threats and take the fangs out of radical Islam.

But should we fear terrorists? What, exactly, is terrorism? One dictionary defines it as "the use of violent acts to frighten the people in an area as a way of trying to achieve a political goal."[12] It would be more accurate to say that terrorism includes not only the use of violence to instill fear in people, but also the reference to threats of potential violent acts. Our conventional interpretation of this term finds application primarily (and sometimes exclusively) in international situations—people tend to believe that terrorism occurs when somebody in one country attacks, or threatens to attack, a group of people in a different country. Ask somebody to describe to you what a terrorist looks like and most of your responses will be in reference to a cave-dwelling Arab wearing a turban. But the definition of the term does not apply geography in this way. While it notes that terrorism is an attempt to frighten people in a given area (such as a city or country), it makes no distinction as to whether the terrorism is foreign or domestic. Indeed, many terrorist acts are committed by a person against those in his own city or country; the political goals terrorists hope to realize often deal with the government under which they themselves live.

Jefferson said that we can't be both ignorant and free, and he was right. Ignorance regarding the nature of terrorism, the reasons and context behind modern-day terrorist acts, and the true identity of terrorists (hint: it's not just the cave-dwelling Arabs) leads people to draw the wrong conclusions and therefore support policies that diminish their freedom. Americans were told in the wake of 9/11 that terrorists "who don't believe in democracy"[13] attacked America "not for our vices, but for our virtues,"[14] that they "reject basic human values and hate the United States and everything for which it stands,"[15] and that they "want to change our ways."[16]

President Bush claimed that terrorists "hate our freedoms: our freedom of religion, our freedom of speech, our freedom to vote and assemble and disagree with each other,"[17] and that "America was targeted for attack because we're the brightest beacon for freedom and opportunity in the world."[18] This narrative, quickly cemented into the psyche of hundreds of millions of individuals, had as its goal the intentional ignorance of the American people. William Blum, author of *Rogue State: A Guide to the World's Only Superpower*, explains:

This *idée fixe*—that the rise of anti-American terrorism owes nothing to American policies—in effect postulates an America that is always the aggrieved innocent in a treacherous world, a benign United States government peacefully going about its business but being "provoked" into taking extreme measures to defend its people, its freedom and its democracy. There consequently is no good reason to modify U.S. foreign policy, and many people who might otherwise know better are scared into supporting the empire's wars out of the belief that there's no choice but to crush without mercy—or even without evidence—this irrational international force out there that hates the United States with an abiding passion.[19]

Politicians and pundits were silent about the truth surrounding these attacks, withholding the history and context necessary to understand why they occurred, in order to further their agenda. That agenda included policies and interventions that were themselves part of the reason America had been attacked. For example, Osama bin Laden wrote a "letter to the American people" articulating the reasons behind the 9/11 attack. Rather than opposition to freedom, culture, and virtue, he explained that his supporters were fighting us "because you attacked us and continue to attack us."[20] He continued: "Your forces occupy our countries; you spread your military bases throughout them; you corrupt our lands, and you besiege our sanctities, to protect the security of the Jews and to ensure the continuity of your pillage of our treasures."

The American people were largely denied access to this perspective and context, thus allowing the prevailing narrative to continue. The Bush administration had asked media outlets in the United States to self-censor bin Laden's letter and other interviews, for fear that they might contain hidden messages. "At best," said White House spokesman Ari Fleischer, "Osama bin Laden's message is propaganda, calling on people to kill Americans. At worst, he could be issuing orders to his followers to initiate such attacks."[21] Fifty-three percent of Americans polled by the Pew Research Center agreed that the censorship was legitimate to help protect national security.[22] But for all its radicalness, bin Laden's reasoning was agreed upon, in general, by the United States government. A Department of Defense study in 1997 concluded, "Historical data show a strong correlation between US involvement in international situations and an increase in terrorist attacks against the United States."[23] In other words, it has long been known that interventions—such as those listed by bin Laden—anger those affected and provoke them to fight back. The CIA has a term for this: blowback. Chalmers Johnson, author of a book by that name, explains:

> "Blowback" is a CIA term first used in March 1954 in a recently declassified report on the 1953 operation to overthrow the government of Mohammad Mossadegh in Iran. It is a metaphor for the unintended consequences of the US government's international activities that have been kept secret from the American people. The CIA's fears that there might ultimately be some blowback from its egregious interference in the affairs of Iran were well founded. Installing the Shah in power brought twenty-five years of tyranny and repression to the Iranian people and elicited the Ayatollah Khomeini's revolution. The staff of the American embassy in Teheran was held hostage for more than a year. This misguided "covert operation" of the US government helped convince many capable people throughout the Islamic world that the United States was an implacable enemy.[24]

Contrary to what is claimed by those in power, one expert on suicide terrorist attacks writes, "The central objective of every suicide terrorist campaign since 1980 has been to compel a democratic state with military forces on territory that the terrorists prize to take those forces out."[25] The average American voter is profoundly ignorant regarding the history of interventions abroad that give rise to retaliatory attacks. When these attacks occur, as shown previously, politicians and pundits do not provide the necessary context because it would implicate them, to some degree, in provoking the attacks. Lacking this data, then, the public largely supports the proposals put forward by those in government to "seek justice" for an attack. These proposals usually entail some form of intervention, purportedly to attack up-and-coming terrorists "on their own soil"[26] and thus the very policies that led to the original attack are once more endorsed, perpetuating a cycle in which fear plays a central role. In these situations, government becomes a disease masquerading as its own cure.

This is the threat posed by ignorance and the sad reality that has resulted from silence about truth. The consequence of ignorance is not only suffering and death for faceless masses half a world away, but a corresponding loss of freedom at home as well. The day of the 9/11 attacks, Representative Ron Paul took to the floor of Congress to sound this prophetic warning:

> Demanding domestic security in times of war invites carelessness in preserving civil liberties and the right of privacy. Frequently the people are only too anxious for their freedoms to be sacrificed on the altar of authoritarianism thought to be necessary to remain safe and secure. Nothing would please the terrorists more than if we willingly give up some of our cherished liberties while defending ourselves from their threat.[27]

Sadly, this is precisely what happened. Crippled by fear of another terrorist attack, Americans supported a variety of policies that were not only problematic in their international implications, but violative of the liberties that government was created to protect. In the name of preventing another airplane attack, Americans were subjected to invasive pat downs, radiational scanning, an increased law enforcement presence, restrictions on what could be carried onboard a plane, and confiscation of harmless, everyday objects such as water bottles and knitting needles. In the name of identifying potential attacks, the government began bulk data collection on innocent Americans, including their phone records, emails, social media posts, instant messages, bank information, and raw internet traffic. To allegedly gain information that might help prevent future terrorist attacks, Americans are now subject to indefinite detention and even targeted assassination at the president's say-so, merely by being classified as an enemy combatant. It can safely be argued that the major policy changes in the post-9/11 era have been detrimental to liberty.

"Once we roared like lions for liberty," observed Norman Vincent Peale. "Now we bleat like sheep for security."[28] Lions are ferocious—not feckless. Sheep, on the other hand, are dumb animals with a strong herd mentality and a willingness to follow a leader—even if that leader is taking them off a cliff. Left alone, sheep are prone to wander in a directionless fashion, oblivious to the threats around them. Ignorance, whether it is willful or intentionally caused, prevents us from making rational decisions, based on knowledge, to respond to actual threats. It allows for leaders with ulterior motives to lead the flock astray—or, as in the case with the boy who cried wolf, lead others astray. Fear leads to enslavement, and as Ralph Waldo Emerson said, "Fear always springs from ignorance."[29] If we are concerned about what fear can do to us—and how others can prey upon us by creating conditions in which that fear is amplified and exploited—then we should make every attempt to become informed.

NOTES

1. Ayn Rand, *Atlas Shrugged* (New York: Signet, 1985), 957.
2. "Witnesses describe atrocities by Iraqis," The Commercial Appeal, October 11, 1990.
3. "Remember Nayirah, Witness for Kuwait?," *The New York Times*, January 6, 1992.
4. "How PR Sold the War in the Persian Gulf," PR Watch, accessed August 2, 2014, http://www.prwatch.org/books/tsigfy10.html.
5. Robin Andersen, *A Century of Media, A Century of War* (New York: Peter Lang Publishing, Inc., 2006), 170.
6. "The Powell Doctrine," *The Harvard Crimson*, September 19, 1995, accessed August 2, 2014, http://www.thecrimson.com/article/1995/9/19/the-powell-doctrine-pwe-are-still/.
7. Troilus and Cressida, Act II, Scene III.
8. Aldous Huxley, *Brave New World* (New York: HarperCollins Publishers, Inc., 2005), 11.
9. "Polls Continue to Show Majority of Americans Against NSA Spying," Electronic Frontier Foundation, January 22, 2014, accessed August 2, 2014, https://www.eff.org/deeplinks/2013/10/polls-continue-show-majority-americans-against-nsa-spying.
10. "ODNI Releases Statistical Transparency Report Regarding Use of National Security Authorities," Office of the Director of National Intelligence, June 27, 2014, accessed August 2, 2014, http://www.dni.gov/index.php/newsroom/reports-and-publications/204-reports-publications-2014/1084-odni-releases-statistical-transparency-report-regarding-use-of-national-security-authorities.
11. Letter to Charles Yancey, January 6, 1816.
12. "Terrorism," Merriam-Webster, accessed August 2, 2014, http://www.merriam-webster.com/dictionary/terrorism.
13. Karen DeYoung, *Soldier: The Life of Colin Powell* (New York: Vintage Books, 2006), 340.

14. "Conservative 'patriots' target liberal academics," *The Guardian*, December 19, 2001, accessed August 2, 2014, http://www. theguardian.com/world/2001/dec/19/worlddispatch. internationaleducationnews.

15. "National Security Strategy of the United States," George W. Bush, September 17, 2002.

16. William Blum, *Rogue State: A Guide to the World's Only Superpower* (Monroe: Common Courage Press, 2005), 30.

17. "Text: President Bush Addresses the Nation," *The Washington Post*, September 20, 2001, accessed August 2, 2014, http://www. washingtonpost.com/wp-srv/nation/specials/attacked/transcripts/ bushaddress_092001.html.

18. "Bush addresses nation: Full text," BBC News, September 12, 2011, accessed August 2, 2014, http://news.bbc.co.uk/2/hi/ americas/1539328.stm.

19. Rogue State, 30.

20. "Full text: bin Laden's 'letter to America'," *The Guardian*, November 24, 2022, accessed August 2, 2014, http://www.theguardian.com/ world/2002/nov/24/theobserver.

21. "Networks Agree to Limit al Qaeda Broadcasts," ABC News, October 10, 2002, accessed August 2, 2014, http://abcnews.go.com/ US/story?id=92343.

22. "Terror Coverage Boost News Media's Images," Pew Research Center for the People & the Press, November 28, 2001, accessed August 2, 2014, http://www.people-press.org/2001/11/28/terror-coverage- boost-news-medias-images/.

23. "Protecting the Homeland: The Best Defense Is to Give No Offense," CATO, May 5, 1998, accessed August 2, 2014, http://www. cato.org/pubs/pas/pa-306.html.

24. "Blowback," The Nation, September 27, 2001, accessed August 2, 2014, http://www.thenation.com/article/blowback.

25. "Why the bombers are so angry at us," The Age, July 23, 2005, accessed August 2, 2014, http://www.theage.com.au/news/opinion/

why-the-bombers-are-so-angry-at-us/2005/07/22/1121539145036. html.

26. "U.S. Training Elite Antiterror Troops in Four African Nations," *The New York Times,* May 26, 2014, accessed August 2, 2014, http:// www.nytimes.com/2014/05/27/world/africa/us-trains-african-commandos-to-fight-terrorism.html.

27. *United States of America Congressional Record: Proceedings and Debates of the 107th Congress, First Session* (Washington: United States Government Printing Office), 16771.

28. Lloyd Cory, ed., *Quote Unquote* (Victor Books: 1977), 180.

29. Ralph Waldo Emerson, *The American Scholar: An Address* (New York: The Laurentian Press, 1901), 40.

THE CALM OF DESPOTISM

"Man is born free, and everywhere he is in chains."[1]
—*Jean-Jacques Rousseau*

TIMID MEN… PREFER THE CALM OF DESPOTISM to the tempestuous sea of liberty," wrote Thomas Jefferson.[2] Fearful people seek security over liberty—they want to be kept safe at almost any expense. Knowing this human reaction, those who desire power and gain exploit it to great success. Thus "the whole aim of practical politics" becomes, as Mencken said, "to keep the populace alarmed (and hence clamorous to be led to safety) by menacing it with an endless series of hobgoblins, most of them imaginary." Of course, real threats exist, and there are people in our neighborhood or around the world who wish to do us harm. Security is therefore important, but too often it comes at the expense of liberty and fundamental rights. As Judge Andrew Napolitano wrote, "Our present government has made every attempt to thwart our right to due process, using claims of national security and state secrets to mask the use of truly dictatorial powers and procedures, profoundly contrary to the natural law."[3]

It is not only the present government that is guilty of despotic acts perpetrated through the use of fear. Certainly the Federalist empowerment of the federal government, through the Alien and Sedition Acts, matches this description. Or consider Abraham Lincoln, a popular president idolized by many, though fully understood by few. As president, Lincoln used the force of the government to shut down newspapers and seize telegraph lines he believed were a threat to the success of his war against the southern states, and imprisoned dozens of their owners and publishers. He imprisoned thousands of Northern citizens without trial, suspended habeas corpus (a prisoner's right, dating back to the 13th century, to contest his imprisonment before a judge), launched a military invasion without the consent of Congress, and persecuted his political critics. Congressman Clement Vallandigham of Ohio objected to this abuse of authority and openly condemned it. He also called for Lincoln's impeachment for his flagrant and frequent violations of the Constitution, which he had taken an oath to uphold. In an 1862 speech, Vallandigham explained his position further:

> No matter how distasteful constitutions and laws
> may be, they must be obeyed. I am opposed to all mobs,
> and opposed also… to all violations of [the C]onstitution
> and law[s] by men in authority—public servants. The
> danger from usurpations and violations by them is fifty-
> fold greater than from any other quarter, because these
> violations and usurpations come clothed with [a] false
> semblance of authority.[4]

Several months later, apparently tired of this open criticism of his actions, Lincoln ordered Union General Ambros Burnside to use his troops to break into Vallandigham's home, arrest him, and transport him to Cincinnati for trial. Their mission was successful, and as a result, a former Congressman was held, without bail, inside a military prison "for no other offense," he wrote to his fellow Ohioans, "than my political opinions and the defense of them, and of the rights of the people, and of your constitutional liberties."[5] Despite Lincoln's unconstitutional violation of habeas corpus, Vallandigham still made the attempt and petitioned a federal court in Ohio for his release, arguing that he was not in the military and therefore not subject to their authority either for his arrest or trial. His request was denied, and he was subsequently convicted by a military tribunal appointed by General Burnside for "declaring disloyal sentiments and opinions, with the object and purpose of weakening the power of the Government in its efforts to suppress an unlawful rebellion."[6] When Vallandigham was sentenced to life imprisonment, Lincoln unilaterally altered the punishment and deported him instead.

Vallandigham's supporters reacted quickly, and rioting ensued in Dayton, Ohio. General Burnside declared martial law, and for good measure shut down the *Dayton Empire*, a newspaper that supported Vallandigham's opposition to Lincoln's actions with such headlines as "Will free men submit? The hour for action has arrived." Controversy continued in the following days, including thousands of people protesting in New York City. In that state, Governor Horatio Seymour—a member of Lincoln's own political party—wrote a letter to Vallandigham's supporters saying, in part:

> Having given [Lincoln's administration] a generous support in the conduct of the war, we pause to see what kind of government it is for which we are asked to pour out our blood and our treasure. The action of the Administration will determine... whether this war is waged to put down rebellion at the South, or destroy free institutions at the North.[7]

For his part, Abraham Lincoln defended his violations of liberty and due process on grounds of exigency and public safety. Vallandigham was arrested and deported, Lincoln wrote, "because he was laboring, with some effect, to prevent the raising of troops;

to encourage desertions from the army; and to leave the rebellion without an adequate military force to suppress it." Of course, free speech is worthless if one can only say or write things that will have no effect or influence. But Lincoln and his supporters were adamant that their war justified a restriction of rights and a suspension of due process because, as Lincoln himself argued before Congress, "the public safety does require"[8] it. Here we see the clashing sides of the spectrum between security and liberty, with Lincoln, in this case, pitting the two against one another and siding with security. A great orator, Lincoln was careful in his use of fear, dealing primarily in abstract terms. Northerners were rallied to war against their southern brethren not to defend themselves, but because of an ill-defined need to defend the Union; "A house divided against itself cannot stand," as Lincoln claimed. The purported consequences of southern secession were not necessarily understood by the common man, though it was feverishly held up as a nation-ending action that must be thwarted, no matter the cost. But in one speech—his first "State of the Union" address before Congress in 1861—Lincoln cited a potential "end game" which would stoke fear into the hearts of those whose parents and grandparents had suffered through military conflict instigated by foreign nations in previous decades: "A nation which endures factious domestic division is exposed to disrespect abroad, and one party, if not both, is sure sooner or later to invoke foreign intervention."[9] To avert international war, Lincoln started his own.

Whatever your opinions on this war or any other, what's non-debatable is the fact that despotic acts almost always accompany wartime measures. Every infringement of liberty is excused, in exigent circumstances, as a necessity without which great peril would certainly result. But not every despotic act takes place during war—after all, Jefferson referred to the *calm* of despotism, and war is anything but calm. Because fear is used as a weapon in cases of physical threats, real or imagined, it's most notable in terrorism or foreign policy issues. Other things affect our physical security, however, such as economic uncertainty. Unemployment and inflation don't carry with them the same urgency—and invoke the same level of fear—as anthrax or a commandeered airplane, but they are a constant threat to millions of individuals who fear being unable to provide basic necessities for themselves and their families.

The constant concern regarding economic stability has led despots throughout history to use it as pretext for centralization and control. The average American would regard the Soviet Union, for example, as a perfect example of using fear to achieve political goals and enacting tyrannical policies that violate liberty. Its 1936 Constitution listed several "fundamental rights" relative to economic comfort and care. What few realize is that politicians within the United States of America were promoting these same entitlements at the same time. President Franklin D. Roosevelt, in his State of the Union address in 1944, called for "the right to adequate protection from the economic fears of old age, sickness, accident, and unemployment" whereas the USSR Constitution declared that its citizens "have the right to maintenance in old age and also in case of sickness or loss of capacity to work." FDR called for the "right to a useful and remunerative job," just as the USSR guaranteed "right to employment." FDR wanted "the right to earn enough to provide adequate food and clothing and recreation" while the USSR declared "the right to rest and leisure." Americans supposedly had the right "to a decent home" and "adequate medical care" while their Soviet counterparts had the "rights to housing" and "the right to health protection."

Each of these entitlements was predicated on a fear: the fear of privation, homelessness, unemployment, and so on. In 1935, for example, the Social Security Act was pushed through Congress as an attempt to shield Americans from dangers associated with old age, poverty, and unemployment. It was, in Roosevelt's words, an attempt "to increase the security... of a larger number of people... to give them assurance that they are not going to starve in their old age."[10] One of the Act's cheerleaders in the Senate argued that it "achieves in the largest measure found possible the ideal of our great President of banishing the gaunt specter of need in old age."[11] Wrapped in emotional rhetoric such as this, the Act passed the House of Representatives 372-33, passed the Senate 77-6, and was cheerfully signed into law by Roosevelt who proclaimed that millions of Americans would finally be able to "reap direct benefits through unemployment compensation, through old-age pensions and through increased services for the protection of children and the prevention of ill health."[12]

This, too, is despotism; fear of life's ever-present uncertainties leads people to support policies that violate liberty and the conniving politicians that promote them. It's easy to equate clearly identified tyrants with tyranny, such as Joseph Stalin and his communist entitlement and central planning economic systems, but it's more difficult for most people to associate tyrannical actions with democratically elected leaders in our day who look and talk like us. But so-called "leaders" throughout history have all claimed that the security of their subjects was their job, be they Roman emperors, kings and queens, revolutionary dictators, or American presidents. James Madison once wrote that Americans "owe their independence and their liberty to the wisdom of descrying [detecting] in the minute tax of 3 pence on tea, the magnitude of the evil comprised in the precedent."[13] In other words, in a relatively insignificant level of taxation, colonists nevertheless recognized the inherent despotism and rejected it. Madison's counsel, based on that reaction and its consequences, is for us to "exert the same wisdom, in watching against every evil lurking under plausible disguises, and growing up from small beginnings."

We're all familiar with the "slippery slope" metaphor or the related proverb of the camel's nose: "If the camel once gets his nose in the tent, his body will soon follow." Despotism is occasionally imposed through bold actions, but has historically proven more successful through incrementalism. At its beginning, for example, the Social

Security tax rate was two percent on the first $3,000 of income, and has since ballooned into a 12.4% tax on the first $117,000 of income. Wars are introduced to nervous electorates as being quick operations before they expand into long conflicts; Defense Secretary Donald Rumsfeld, arguing that the war in Iraq would not become a quagmire, opined that military operations would only be "five days or five weeks or five months, but it certainly isn't going to last any longer than that."[14] Surveillance operations, to the extent they're publicly known, are justified as necessary against foreign threats while, often behind the scenes, they are used domestically. "Once things have gone so far," wrote F.A. Hayek in *The Road to Serfdom*, "liberty indeed becomes almost a mockery, since it can be purchased only by the sacrifice of most of the good things of the earth."[15]

But despotism doesn't involve the forceful violation of liberty on the part of the tyrant—too often that liberty is freely surrendered by those who desire security, be it physical, economic, emotional, or otherwise. Forty percent of Americans polled just before the 10th anniversary of 9/11 agreed that "in order to curb terrorism in this country it will be necessary for the average person to give up some civil liberties."[16] A week after the Boston Marathon attack, in which surveillance camera footage helped identify the suspects, 78% of Americans polled said that it would be a "good idea" to augment the surveillance state in hopes of deterring terrorism.[17] Americans are bleating like sheep for security and, as a result, are following leaders down dangerous paths of despotism.

ENABLING TYRANNY

Susie Castillo was traveling from Rio de Janeiro to Los Angeles on April 21, 2011. Her international trip required her to go through a security screening in Dallas, Texas. After objecting to the TSA agent's request for her to stand inside a full body scanner, Castillo was subjected to a pat down. After the agent found no explosive materials or other contraband on Castillo, she walked a few steps and then turned on her cell phone to record her emotional reaction:

> I'm sure this woman was just doing her job. But she, I mean she actually felt—touched—my vagina. And so I think that's why I'm crying, that's why I'm so emotional, because I'm already so upset that they're making me do this—making me choose to either get molested, because that's what I feel like, or go through this machine that's completely unhealthy and dangerous. I don't want to go through it, and here I am crying.[18]

In its predictable response to Castillo's subsequent complaint, the TSA told media outlets, "We have reviewed this passenger's screening experience and found that the officer followed proper procedures." Castillo was right: the TSA agent patting her down, and touching the most intimate parts of her body, was "just doing her job." The TSA further pointed out that of the 252 million people screened at airport checkpoints between November 2010 and March 2011, only 898 complaints had been filed with the agency from individuals who experienced a pat down.

The fear of an aircraft hijacking led to a variety of despotic and reactionary policies, including the requirement to be subjected to invasive searches and seizures. That so few objected is both predictable and depressing. What's worse is that many welcomed this supposed security measure, if for nothing else than to be comforted by the psychological effect it had on them, helping them to feel safer. Those who objected were almost always told that their experience was "by the book" and that the agents were not only "just doing their job"—they were doing their job well.

Politicians who propose policies such as this, and pundits who generate support for them, cannot act alone. Even after the public is convinced of the necessity of surrendering their liberty in the quest for security, somebody has to actually implement the policy. Despots need obedient subordinates to execute political opponents, imprison dissidents, fight protesters, collect taxes, and harass the citizenry. Indeed, they cannot be despots *unless* they are able to command countless other human beings to follow their orders. Whether democratically elected or not, those who exercise tyrannical power are at the mercy of those who decide whether to listen to them. Evil triumphs, as Edmund Burke observed, when good men do nothing.

Soldiers kill innocent people; NSA agents invade our privacy; police officers shut down lemonade stands; central bankers erode the savings of senior citizens; medical marijuana patients are incarcerated; legislators vote away more of our money—these and a list of wrongful acts too lengthy to fit in this book are regularly perpetrated by persons clothed in the authority of the state. They are, we must suppose, sincere people with good intentions and families to feed. We are told that they are just doing their job, and that if we have any complaint we should take it up with the authorities—those who determine the policies these people enforce.

Recall that James Madison's suggestion was to identify evil lurking under disguise with small beginnings. Consider a grievous and well known example of evil neither well disguised nor small: the extermination of millions of Jews under the orders of Adolf Hitler and his Nazi subordinates. The gravity of this crisis often leads to a series of simple yet profound questions: why didn't anybody stop it? Why didn't people speak out and resist Hitler's policy proposals as they escalated, bit by bit, into mass genocide?

These were the questions pondered by Milton Mayer, author of *They Thought They Were Free: The Germans, 1933-45*. "As an American, I was repelled by the rise of National Socialism in Germany," Mayer wrote. "As an American of German descent, I was ashamed. As a Jew, I was stricken. As a newspaperman, I was fascinated." The author attempted to understand how Germans "got that way" in hopes that this information would serve as a learning opportunity for his own countrymen. He tried for a month, without success, to meet with Adolf Hitler in 1935 and pick his brain. Writing two decades later in summary of his research, Mayer said:

> I saw the German people, people I had known when I visited Germany as a boy, and for the first time realized that Nazism was a mass movement and not the tyranny of a diabolical few over helpless millions. Then I wondered if Adolf Hitler was, after all, the Nazi I wanted to see. By the time the war was over I had identified my man: the average German...
>
> Now I see a little better how Nazism overcame Germany—not by attack from without or by subversion from within, but with a whoop and a holler. It was what most Germans wanted—or, under pressure of combined reality and illusion, came to want. They wanted it; they got it; and they liked it.[19]

Mayer found an alarming aspect of humanity in the Germans who supported the Nazi regime: they were normal people, like you and me, who were persuaded of the necessity of the policies they obeyed, "at first awkwardly but, surprisingly soon, spontaneously."[20] The masses became not reluctant participants, but active cheerleaders. "I came back home a little afraid for my country," Mayer wrote, "afraid of what it might want, and get, and like, under pressure of combined reality and illusion. I felt—and feel—that it was not German Man that I had met, but Man. He happened to be in Germany under certain conditions. He might be here, under certain conditions. He might, under certain conditions, be I."[21]

James Madison noted that evil starts small and in disguise, and such was the case in Germany; the purported purification of the Aryan race was not the Nazi party's first proposal. Austria was a free country but full of unemployed people and political turmoil.

In strode Adolf Hitler, inundating the people with promises of a better life, if only Austria were annexed to Germany and he were elected. Hitler has been branded, in hindsight, as a vicious tyrant, and rightly so—but he rose to power as a charismatic visionary subtly preying on people's fears and claiming the ability to provide them with "calm." Government jobs were created and order was restored; people were hopeful and happy—at least for a short time. Then came gun registration, socialized medicine, nationalization of education, central control of businesses, mandatory work for women outside the home, daycare indoctrination centers for the children, and so on. "What no one seemed to notice," said one German in Mayer's book, "was the ever widening gap, after 1933, between the government and the people." He continued:

> What happened here was the gradual habituation of the people, little by little, to being governed by surprise; to receiving decisions deliberated in secret; to believing that the situation was so complicated that the government had to act on information which the people could not understand, or so dangerous that, even if the people could understand it, it could not be released because of national security...
>
> This separation of government from the people, this widening of the gap, took place so gradually and so insensibly, each step disguised (perhaps not even intentionally) as a temporary emergency measure or associated with true patriotic allegiance or with real social purposes. And all the crises and reforms (real reforms, too) so occupied the people that they did not see the slow motion underneath, of the whole process of government growing remoter and remoter.[22]

But still, we must speculate, there were surely people along the way who saw what was happening and attempted to do something about it. If evil triumphs when good men do nothing, did evil succeed so boldly in Germany because there were no good men, or at least none who attempted to speak out? Reading the interviews and journals of those who stood by silently, or participated cheerfully, reveals the effects of fear when it permeates an entire culture—political institutions erected through fear, programs enforced through fear, and people conditioned to fear. Many in the group that supported these policies did so because they feared losing their culture, their political power, or their economic stability. This fear was eagerly exploited by the despots-in-waiting who promised to keep them safe and secure in the status quo (though clearly, this did not occur). Another part of the group—those who did observe problems but failed to do anything about them—were often crippled by fear of rebuke, unemployment, public shame, or death. How could they not fear this result? The Nazi regime regularly executed dissidents, killing some 77,000 Germans for political offenses by the war's end, along with around 25,000 German soldiers.[23] There was a very real, raw reason to keep quiet. Many good Germans, however, simply were unable to comprehend the true nature of the threat. One of them, interviewed by Mayer, explained this condition in detail and deserves to be quoted at length:

> [O]ne doesn't see exactly where or how to move. Believe me, this is true. Each act, each occasion, is worse than the last, but only a little worse. You wait for the next and the next. You wait for one great shocking occasion, thinking that others, when such a shock comes, will join with you in resisting somehow. You don't want to act, or even talk, alone; you don't want to "go out of your way to make trouble." Why not?—Well, you are not in the habit of doing it. And it is not just fear, fear of standing alone, that restrains you; it is also genuine uncertainty.

But the one great shocking occasion, when tens or hundreds or thousands will join with you, never comes. That's the difficulty. If the last and worst act of the whole regime had come immediately after the first and smallest, thousands, yes, millions would have been sufficiently shocked—if, let us say, the gassing of the Jews in '43 had come immediately after the "German Firm" stickers on the windows of non-Jewish shops in '33. But of course this isn't the way it happens. In between come all the hundreds of little steps, some of them imperceptible, each of them preparing you not to be shocked by the next. Step C is not so much worse than Step B, and, if you did not make a stand at Step B, why should you at Step C? And so on to Step D.

And one day, too late, your principles, if you were ever sensible of them, all rush in upon you. The burden of self-deception has grown too heavy, and some minor incident, in my case my little boy, hardly more than a baby, saying "Jewish swine," collapses it all at once, and you see that everything—everything—has changed, and changed completely under your nose. The world you live in—your nation, your people—is not the world you were born in at all. The forms are all there, all untouched, all reassuring, the houses, the shops, the jobs, the mealtimes, the visits, the concerts, the cinema, the holidays. But the spirit, which you never noticed because you made the lifelong mistake of identifying it with the forms, is changed. Now you live in a world of hate and fear, and the people who hate and fear do not even know it themselves; when everyone is transformed, no one is transformed. Now you live in a system which rules without responsibility even to God. The system itself could not have intended this in the beginning, but in order to sustain itself it was compelled to go all the way.[24]

This is the tragic result of people "just doing their job," either conditioned or crippled by fear. This is the consequence of failing to identify and reject small, disguised but despotic acts. This is what happens when one's conscience is repeatedly compromised. "Suddenly it all comes down, all at once," added Mayer's German friend. "You see what you are, what you have done, or, more accurately, what you haven't done (for that was all that was required of most of us: that we do nothing)… You remember everything now, and your heart breaks. Too late. You are compromised beyond repair."

Tyranny only succeeds to the extent that a complicit citizenry supports it. Unfortunately, as psychological experiments have shown, it is human nature to submit one's conscience to authority, and as a result people "just do their job" even when their task entails violating the rights, or even taking the life, of another. The "Milgram Experiment," which has been repeated many times in different societies with consistent results, involves creating an environment where participants are instructed to perform acts that violate their conscience—usually the administration of a series of electric shocks upon a person in another room, whom they cannot see but can hear. Each shock, the participant is told, is more powerful and painful than the last, until a final, fatal voltage is delivered. Of course, no pain is actually inflicted upon the unseen person, but the participant does not know this and can hear his screams of agony. The experiments first began in July 1961, three months after the trial of Nazi war criminal Adolf Eichmann commenced. Milgram sought to answer the question we have been reviewing: "Could it be that Eichmann and his million accomplices in the Holocaust were just following orders? Could we call them all accomplices?"[25] No matter where this experiment has been conducted, the results have shown that 61 to 66 percent of participants inflict the fatal voltage upon the other person when instructed to do so by the authority figure.

It remains to be seen how—or if—individuals can break free from this trend, act in accordance with what their conscience tells them, and question—and where necessary, reject—authority. Incremental infringements on our liberties, right up to the greatest atrocities the world has seen, have been perpetrated by masses of automaton-like people who were "just doing their job." Certainly there is a measure of understanding to be had for good people who act (or don't act) due to fear and ignorance. But whatever the level of individual culpability, the systemic result of widespread fear is clear and cautionary, as so many, having been promised comfort and calm, have found themselves under despotic rule, resulting in the total destruction of liberty and, in many tragic cases, death.

PROPAGANDA

In December 2010, 26-year-old Mohamed Bouazizi was selling produce at a roadside stand in a rural town in Tunisia, where he had worked for seven years, providing for a widowed mother and six siblings as the family's sole breadwinner. Due to his lack of a permit, a policewoman confiscated his cart and produce, and when Bouazizi attempted to pay the fine, the policewoman insulted his deceased father and allegedly slapped him. Afterward, Bouazizi visited the provincial headquarters to file a complaint but was turned away. Within an hour of the initial confrontation at the roadside stand, he proceeded to drench himself with a flammable liquid and set himself on fire. This act of desperation sparked a firestorm of protests from sympathetic Tunisians, catalyzing civil unrest and opposition that had been bubbling beneath the surface for years.

Tunisia's president had been in power for 23 years, reigning over a government riddled with corruption and crackdowns on dissenters and political opponents. Motivated by these and other issues, such as high unemployment, inflated food prices, and poor living conditions, citizens poured into the streets en masse—activists, students, professors, lawyers, and a variety of other groups—to call for the president's resignation. A popular chant was "We are not afraid, we are not afraid, we are afraid only of God."[26] Four weeks after Bouazizi's self-immolation sparked a countrywide revolt, the president stepped down and fled to Saudi Arabia. Revolts continued, leading the way towards a government shake-up though progress has been slow, and most of the problems that led to revolution remain.

The success of the Tunisian uprising inspired activists and discontented citizens in neighboring nations, resulting in a wave of opposition throughout almost all the Arab countries—the "Arab Spring." Just one month after Tunisia's president was toppled, Egyptian president Hosni Mubarak resigned, ending his brutal 30-year presidency. Major protests then broke out in Libya and turned into a full-blown civil war, resulting in the downfall of Muammar Gaddafi's repressive 42-year regime a few months later. Several other heads of state stepped down from power or announced they would not seek re-election, offering a glimpse of hope to those who for years—or their entire lives, in many cases—had been living under oppressive political establishments.

There are some who might look at these dethroned despots and consider them amateurs for having carelessly created circumstances that led to their loss of political power. Thomas Jefferson had observed timid men who preferred not confrontational despotism, but *calm* despotism—a result that requires precision and careful execution. The despotism with which we generally associate the term enrages those who clearly see the injury being caused them, whether it be a friend brutally punished by the police, a relative tortured for his political opposition, or a job lost due to harsh economic controls.

"I consider that in no government power can be abused long," wrote Samuel Johnson, the famous 18th-century British literary figure. "Mankind will not bear it. If a sovereign oppresses his people to a great degree, they will rise and cut off his head. There is a remedy in human nature against tyranny, that will keep us safe under every form of government."[27] He was referring, of course, to the typical form of despotism with which the world has been all too familiar—the form that certainly has taken shape for decades in the authoritarian regimes that litter the Middle East. But what of calm despotism? As explained previously, this refers to a situation in which tyrannical policies are imposed upon people who welcome and embrace them cheerfully—a situation catalyzed by and capitalized upon through fear. Under this scenario, the loss of freedom is either not noticed or too little felt. Just as a person who believes his life is in peril due to an imminent attack is not likely to pay much attention to a stomach ache, so too do people disregard the violation of their liberty by spending their time, attention, and energy upon perceived threats to their very lives. This political sleight of hand has proven very effective for those who *aren't* amateurs—despots who realize that the preservation of their power must be done in such a way as to lead people to believe they are (or will be) safe and happy, and that the cost, whatever it might be, is worth it.

Johann Wolfgang von Goethe, the German statesman, once wrote: "None are more hopelessly enslaved than those who falsely believe they are free."[28] Successful despots create circumstances in which people voluntarily surrender their power, primarily through the use of weaponized fear, and those who are masters at their craft are able to accumulate power and wealth while the populace believes it is safe, happy, and free.

This is the domain of propaganda, a psychological tool to manipulate thought and emotion in favor of a certain set of ideas. The word itself simply refers to the propagation of ideas—something to which we can hardly object. Public health notices, religious advocacy, business advertisements, and a host of other common marketing efforts can all be classified as propaganda. But the term has taken on a negative connotation since the mid-19th century, when it became associated with the use of misleading information to achieve political gain. Like fear, propaganda has been weaponized by those who seek to achieve, expand, and retain power over others.

The most popular pioneer of propaganda is Edward Bernays, a nephew of Sigmund Freud, who quite literally wrote the book on the subject, titled *Propaganda*. He called his work the "engineering of consent," asking, "Is it not possible to control and regiment the masses according to our will without their knowing about it? The recent practice of propaganda has proved that it is possible, at least up to a certain point and within certain limits."[29] Bernays was a close confidant of President Woodrow Wilson, and is credited with convincing the American public that the country's war efforts were to "bring democracy to all Europe."

At the Paris Peace Conference in 1919, where the Allied victors set the terms of the cease of hostilities, Bernays joined Wilson, along with representatives from 32 nations. Bernays was impressed by the success of the democracy slogan in swaying public opinion, both domestically and internationally, leading him to wonder how his propaganda model might be employed during peacetime. He started his own consulting business and, due to the negative connotation of the term propaganda, began to promote the new term "public relations." An entire industry was born, and Bernays began shilling for politically connected corporations and other companies, looking to manipulate public opinion in their favor. Cigarettes, bacon, light bulbs, fruit, soap, water fluoridation, sex education—these and a host of other industries benefitted from Bernays' ability to shape the opinions of the masses. His repeated success, both in political and private fields, earned him the title of "professional poisoner of the mind" from a Supreme Court Justice.[30] Out of the many doozies that can be found in Bernays' book *Propaganda*, consider this one:

> The conscious and intelligent manipulation of the organized habits and opinions of the masses is an important element in democratic society. Those who manipulate the organized habits and opinions of the masses constitute an invisible government which is the true ruling power of the country... It remains a fact that in almost every act of our daily lives, whether in the sphere of politics or business, in our social conduct or our ethical thinking, we are dominated by the relatively small number of persons... It is they who pull the wires which control the public mind, who harness old social forces and contrive new ways to bind and guide the world.[31]

Bernays felt that the public "could very easily vote for the wrong man or want the wrong thing, so that they had to be guided from above,"[32] and that capturing the media was key: "If you can influence the leaders, either with or without their conscious cooperation, you automatically influence the group which they sway." His book, building on his series of successes, became a veritable blueprint for cultivating public favor for something that might otherwise be unpopular. It's little surprise, then, that politicians since the Wilsonian progressive era have implemented Bernays' lessons with great success; after all, as Bernays himself said, "Propaganda is the executive arm of the invisible government."[33] Put differently, it is the way by which "calm despotism" can be engineered.

Upon gaining power in 1933, Adolf Hitler established the Reich Ministry of Public Enlightenment and Propaganda. Having previously written about the benefit of propaganda in his 1926 book *Mein Kampf*, Hitler was eager to aggressively implement it and tasked Joseph Goebbels with promoting the Nazi message through art, music, theater, films, books, radio, educational materials, and the press. As documented in the *Holocaust Encyclopedia*:

The Nazi regime used propaganda effectively to mobilize the German population to support its wars of conquest until the very end of the regime. Nazi propaganda was likewise essential to motivating those who implemented the mass murder of the European Jews and of other victims of the Nazi regime. It also served to secure the acquiescence of millions of others—as bystanders—to racially targeted persecution and mass murder.[34]

Edward Bernays later discovered that Goebbels had learned a great deal from *Propaganda*. "Goebbels... was using my book," he wrote, "as a basis for his destructive campaign against the Jews of Germany. This shocked me."[35] Bernays was a very intelligent man, so it is hard to imagine that he was truly shocked that overtly evil people would use the same tactics he had honed and recommended. Whether Bernays was sincerely surprised or not, Goebbels and the Nazi regime definitely made use of the strategies articulated in *Propaganda*—and with great success. Looking past domestic despotism while decrying its implementation internationally is nothing new; hypocrisy is, after all, part of the human condition. Jesus, for example, castigated those who objected to others' motes while ignoring their own beams. In our day, most Americans would likely reject the characterization of their own government as oppressive, while willingly applying the label to foreign nations. It is easy to judge others for their failures and look past our own, especially those of the same type to which we object.

An important rhetorical device within the broader realm of propaganda is the use of repetition to emphasize and reinforce an idea. It is the basis of modern advertising—familiar jingles and commercials that play the same message *ad nauseam* in order to implant an idea into the listener's subconsciousness. But just as repetition is used for commercial purposes, it's also used for political purposes. One example was previously mentioned: the 2004 Republican Convention in which speakers used the same frightening terms over and over to capitalize on fear felt by most Americans. Repetition is often found in political campaigns, with slogans and signs associating in the public's mind the connection of an idea with a candidate. "Hope and change" makes one think immediately of Barack Obama, for instance. In describing the nature of propaganda more generally, and repetition's relationship to it, Goebbels referred to it as

> a carefully built up erection of statements, which whether true or false can be made to undermine quite rigidly held ideas and to construct new ones that will take their place. It would not be impossible to prove with sufficient repetition and psychological understanding of the people concerned that a square is in fact a circle. What after all are a square and a circle? They are mere words and words can be molded until they clothe ideas in disguise.[36]

Repetitive propaganda is widespread; President Bush once said that "In my line of work you got to keep repeating things over and over and over again for the truth to sink in, to kind of catapult the propaganda."[37] Repetition serves both to influence those who are ignorant—imprinting the propagandist's message onto a blank template—as well as those who believe differently, but whose views might be changed through consistent, persuasive propaganda. This latter group is won over through ideological incrementalism, whereby small, steady changes go virtually unnoticed—just as the Germans interviewed by Milton Mayer did not observe the "gradual habituation of the people" in their own country.

Not many years ago, a traveler would have objected to a search and seizure prior to boarding an airplane. However, government mandates have gradually piled on, first requiring the removal of metal belts or accessories, then of shoes, then liquids, then nail clippers, etc., until most people have now become accustomed to stripping down in the middle of an airport in order to be allowed on a plane. Indeed, as government agents run their fingers inside the waistband of travelers' underwear, and in close proximity (if not actual contact) with the person's genitalia, too many believe that the action is somehow necessary for national security. They believe this, of course, because the government has loudly and frequently told them that this is the case. Most Americans love freedom and believe they have it, yet according to Goethe, are "hopelessly enslaved."

Would there be an "American Spring" if somebody acted like the Tunisian merchant Mohamed Bouazizi? Put differently, is there an undercurrent of opposition to the government, awaiting a simple catalyst to engulf the country in revolutionary fervor? One of the key differences between America and Tunisia—the difference between political leaders in the two nations—is the successful use of propaganda to convince Americans they are free, even as their freedoms are gutted from within. As author Michael Parenti has observed, "The enormous gap between what U.S. leaders do in the world and what Americans think their leaders are doing is one of the great propaganda accomplishments of the dominant political mythology."[38] Whether by deliberately repeating falsehoods or by omitting key facts, politicians and pundits persuade the public that the government is "spreading democracy" or liberating an oppressed people, and lead us to give up our essential liberties. "Misrepresentation, false propaganda, innuendoes soon sprout into poisonous weeds," observed David O. McKay, a prominent American religious leader, "and before long the people find themselves victims of a pollution that has robbed them of their individual liberty and enslaved them to a group of political gangsters."[39]

Political candidates routinely use propaganda in their campaigns, almost always exploiting some sort of fear: the fear of what happens if "the other guy" wins, the fear of cuts to precious government programs, the fear of weakness inviting attack, or any number of other contemporary concerns. Perhaps the most famous example is the "Daisy" advertisement used by Lyndon B. Johnson in the 1964 presidential election race against challenger Barry Goldwater. The commercial showed a sweet, two-year-old girl plucking petals off a flower, counting out loud as she removed each one. After several seconds, the viewer heard a military-style countdown and then saw a large explosion, suggesting a nuclear strike. The advertisement concludes with an encouragement to "Vote for President Johnson on November 3. The stakes are too high for you to stay home." While it only aired once, it had its intended effect—it was the subject of conversation on all the news and commentary television programs, and though some analysts criticized Johnson for exploiting the fear of nuclear war for political gain, it worked. The "Daisy" advertisement is considered a significant factor in Johnson's defeat of Goldwater.

Media establishments, of course, are the vehicle for delivering the propaganda—sometimes unintentionally, sometimes deliberately. So-called news agencies can and do shape public opinion both by what they selectively choose to report and by what they decide to exclude. As one example, journalists almost universally disregard stories about people successfully defending themselves with guns. During 2001, *The New York Times* printed 104 news articles on gun-related crimes, for a total of 50,745 words. They printed only one story where a gun was used defensively, for a total of 163 words.[40] *USA Today* devoted 5,660 words to gun-related crimes and zero words for the defensive use of guns. That same year, *The Washington Post* spent 46,884 words describing crimes involving guns, while offering up only 953 words reporting on their use in self-defense. Furthermore, the stories that actually do mention using a gun in self-defense are almost always reported only locally, while the gun-related crime stories often are given national and even international attention. There is clearly a media bias as it relates to reporting on the successful and responsible use of firearms to defend life, liberty, and property. The gun-related stories that are reported are controversial, sometimes tragic, and usually spread fear. Unsurprisingly, they often result in increased support for policies that restrict our right to bear arms, promoted by fearful people hoping to feel safe. Without the context of other stories showing a different point of view, they are persuaded to believe that gun violence is an epidemic requiring drastic action. Two professors who analyzed the use of fear in media wrote, "The prevalence of fear in public discourse can contribute to stances and reactive social policies that promote state control and surveillance."[41] They further concluded:

> Fear pervades popular culture and the news media. Whether used as a noun, verb, adverb, or adjective, an ongoing study finds that the word "fear" pervades news reports across all sections of newspapers, and is shown to move or "travel" from one topic to another. The use of fear and the thematic emphases spawned by entertainment formats are consistent with a "discourse of fear," or the pervasive communication, symbolic awareness and expectation that danger and risk are a central feature of the effective environment... Analysis suggests that this use of fear is consistent with popular culture oriented to pursuing a "problem frame" and entertainment formats, which also have social implications for social policy and reliance on formal agents of social control.[42]

One of the study's authors summarized additional research on the subject as follows:

> The politics of fear is buffered by news and popular culture, stressing fear and threat as features of entertainment that, increasingly, are shaping public and private life as mass-mediated experience and has become a standard frame of reference for audiences, claims-makers, and individual actors. Similar to propaganda, messages about fear are repetitious, stereotypical of outside "threats" and especially suspect and "evil others." These messages also resonate moral panics, with the implication that action

must be taken to not only defeat a specific enemy, but to also save civilization. Since so much is at stake, it follows that drastic measures must be taken, that compromises with individual liberty and even perspectives about "rights", the limits of law, and ethics must be "qualified" and held in abeyance in view of the threat.[43]

Even while many Germans were skeptical of their government's claims, they were still less likely to believe claims made by foreign governments. "All things being equal," wrote Randall Bytwerk, an expert in the nature and use of propaganda, "most people want to believe they live in a good country."[44] When media outlets in foreign nations unquestioningly regurgitate government talking points, Americans call it propaganda. When familiar media institutions here in America do the same, it's somehow considered journalism. Russia Today is a media institution funded entirely by the Russian government; President Putin observed that, as a result, "It cannot help but reflect the Russian government's official position."[45] In July 2014, a London-based correspondent named Sara Firth quit after alleging that she was fed up with seeing reporters repeatedly lie to the public. "We are asked on a daily basis if not to totally ignore than to obscure the truth," she wrote on Twitter.[46] "I couldn't do it any more, we're lying every single day," she later said.[47] "Every single day we're lying and finding sexier ways to do it."

Americans would be quick to object to state ownership of a media company, as in Russia's case, but for decades, the U.S. government has produced media content, which it calls news, to be disseminated internationally. The Broadcasting Board of Governors is a federal agency that oversees the production and distribution of this material using an annual budget of $733 million (provided by American taxpayers), over 3,500 employees, and a nine-member governing board which includes the Secretary of State and eight other individuals appointed by the president. Their content is distributed to 125 markets around the world in 61 different languages through a variety of media companies including Voice of America, Radio Free Europe, Radio Liberty, and the Middle East Broadcasting Networks, among others. Until recently, this content was aimed only at international markets, as early congressional conflict resulted in a domestic ban on the use of this material.[48] At one point, there was an attempt to shut down the operation altogether; Nebraska Senator Edward Zorinsky argued that this "propaganda" should be kept out of America to distinguish the United States "from the Soviet Union where domestic propaganda is a principal government activity." But this program survived its challengers, and is now thriving—the ban on domestic distribution ended on July 2, 2013, opening the door for the government to spread its propaganda to millions of Americans as well.[49]

Of course, propaganda through media does not require a state-owned institution with reporters on the government payroll. Whether through self-censorship, or direct or indirect pressure from government agents, so-called "independent" media institutions can and do likewise convey propaganda. When Israel and Gaza engaged in further conflict in July 2014, NBC's foreign correspondent Ayman Mohyeldin was on the ground reporting events as they occurred—and placing himself and his team at great risk of harm. Stun grenades and rubber bullets were fired at them, as Mohyeldin yelled, "Journalists!" in three languages. For all this raw footage, and relevant reporting, he was given 73 seconds of air time on Brian Williams' evening newscast.[50] Mohyeldin also reported events unfolding in Gaza through social media, and he reported on Twitter that "4 Palestinian kids [were] killed in a single Israeli airstrike. Minutes before they were killed [near] our hotel, I was kicking a ball with them."[51] He proceeded to list their names, and he showed photos of their wailing parents as well as a video of one of the mothers as she learned the news of her son's death. While social media and alternative news outlets exploded at the news of this attack, NBC remained silent; Mohyeldin was nowhere to be seen that evening on Williams' show. Citing security concerns, an NBC executive ordered Mohyeldin to leave Gaza immediately, replacing him with another reporter, Richard Engel, who flew to Israel and did a "report" on the day's events from that country, even though he had only landed one hour prior to his segment.

Evidently, it would seem, "security concerns" were not the real reason for censoring Mohyeldin. A more plausible explanation is that his removal was instigated by his humanization of the war and education of the public on the plight of those in Gaza, who are generally demonized by Western media as terrorists. (This explanation is further supported by the fact that after significant social media opposition to the apparent censorship, NBC reversed course and sent Mohyeldin back to Gaza.) NBC was joined in its censorship of positions contrary to full-fledged American support of Israel by CNN, who removed one of its correspondents from the region the day after Mohyeldin's reassignment by NBC. Diana Magnay was reporting on the ground invasion of the Gaza Strip by Israeli forces, and as missiles flew through the sky behind her, striking buildings (including residences) in Gaza, Israeli spectators surrounding Magnay cheered the bombardment. She later tweeted that some of these individuals had been harassing and threatening her and her crew before and during the report. She wrote on Twitter, "Israelis on hill above Sderot cheer as bombs land on Gaza; threaten to 'destroy our car if I say a word wrong'. Scum."[52] Her tweet was later deleted, and Magnay was sent to Moscow to report on other topics.

Rula Jebreal is an Israeli citizen and a Palestinian journalist who had been a correspondent with MSNBC for two years when the Mohyeldin incident occurred. Upset with his treatment and, more broadly, with the unbalanced coverage given to the pro-Israeli position, Jebreal took to the airwaves to voice her concern. "We are disgustingly biased when it comes to this issue," she said during one of her appearances. "Look how [much] air time [Israeli Prime Minister] Netanyahu and his folks have on air on a daily basis… I never see one Palestinian being interviewed on these same issues."[53]

Following her criticism of her employer and their biased coverage of the conflict, Jebreal's future appearances were canceled and her contract renewal was taken off the table.[54] Commenting on her situation afterward, she mentioned how she had repeatedly protested in private to producers prior to her on-air grievance, "but everybody's intimidated by this pressure, and if it's not direct then it becomes self-censorship," she said.[55] An NBC producer, speaking on condition of anonymity, described "a top-down intimidation campaign aimed at presenting an Israeli-centric view of the attack on the Gaza Strip" with a corresponding "witch hunt" against those, like Jebreal, who didn't toe the propaganda line.[56]

In addition to news media, entertainment is also used to convey propaganda. In 2000, it was revealed that the White House had spent tens of millions of taxpayer dollars paying studios to work anti-drug plots into the scripts of primetime shows; it continued doing so even after criticism and opposition.[57] More recently, similar efforts were made to weave positive references to Barack Obama's signature health care reform proposal into TV shows and movies.[58] With the explosion of social media, governments are also looking for ways to influence people through this new medium. The U.S. Department of Defense spent millions of taxpayer dollars, for example, on its "Social Media in Strategic Communication" project to harvest, categorize, and analyze social media posts on Twitter, Facebook, Pinterest, and Kickstarter.[59] Information released by Edward Snowden suggests that this strategy has been in place for years, with agents of the government engaged in "discrediting" the government's enemies by spreading false information online.[60]

Why is all of this so disturbing? Because information influences belief and behavior, and if our information is not correct, we are likely to make poor, fear-based decisions. Wilton Sekzer, whose son was killed in the World Trade Center towers on 9/11, revered the president and initially supported retaliation against Saddam Hussein's regime, but when he realized that the information he had been basing his beliefs on was wrong, he changed his beliefs, and subsequently changed his actions. Perception management is important to authoritarians who desire to minimize or deny access to information that would harm their re-election efforts, generate opposition to their rule, or otherwise breed discontent amongst the governed masses. For this reason, it's imperative that we do a better job of informing ourselves instead of relying upon government propaganda.

THE PURSUIT OF CALM

While propaganda can exploit a variety of emotions, it is often associated with events or issues that instill fear into the mind of the recipient. This carefully crafted messaging is based upon the natural desire for stability, normalcy, and safety—in other words, calm. Human nature leads us to look with skepticism and consternation on those who "rock the boat" or bring controversial or unpleasant matters to our attention. We therefore tend to support proposals that appear to promote a state of calm. Few care that the system claiming to provide that calm requires destroying the foundations of liberty upon which the entire structure was based.

Let's consider a few examples to see how the desire for calm leads a person to embrace fear-driven propaganda. Much can be said of modern immigration problems, but the genesis of current federal immigration policy is more pertinent to our topic. In the mid-1800s, the Gold Rush seduced people of all nationalities, and Chinese immigrants came in droves to try their hand at mining for riches and to explore other kinds of industry. As things settled down after the fever pitch, many of the Chinese workforce became employed on the Transcontinental Railroad project, competing with American workers for day-laborer jobs. Naturally, this didn't sit well with those who felt entitled to "American jobs." The Chinese as a bloc rapidly became perceived as an economic threat. San Francisco, which by this time had become a multicultural melting pot of its own, was home to a protest in 1870 by American factory workers rallying around the slogan "The Chinese must go!" Popular culture soon embraced a widespread denigration of Chinese immigrants, painting them as strange rat-eaters as well as job-stealers. These pressures led to policy mandates focused precisely on the Chinese population. For example, San Francisco passed an ordinance forbidding people from walking on sidewalks with a pole and baskets over their shoulders (a common practice among the Chinese). Pressure mounted from the western states for the federal government to institute restrictions on immigration. This resulted in an amendment to a treaty that had previously recognized the right of migration, along with congressional changes to fully ban Chinese migration.[61]

While it's easy to see racism or xenophobia as the basis for American opposition to Chinese labor, the real reason for the concerted effort to expel them from the country was economic protectionism. Simply put, a Chinese man willing to work for half the typical American wage was perceived as a threat by Americans who feared losing their jobs to this steep competition. Thus the typical American worker, acting upon this fear, eagerly went along with propaganda that validated and exaggerated this threat, generating political support for reform policies that claimed to address and neutralize it, restoring the previous "calm." While this chapter in American history may be viewed as extreme, as it was accompanied by mobocracy and murders, the same mentality persists today; the fear of economic competition pervades the electorate, and therefore public policy.

The case of Jestina Clayton provides a modern bookend to this longstanding, fear-oriented issue. Growing up in Sierra Leone, Jestina was taught traditional African hair-braiding as a young girl. At the age of 22, she moved to Utah and found a niche market for her unique skills. Jestina started up a hair-braiding business, advertising her services online. A "concerned citizen" who saw her advertisement emailed her: "It is illegal in the state of Utah to do any form of [hair] extensions without a valid cosmetology license. Please delete your ad, or you will be reported."[62] Obtaining such a license would have cost her at least $16,000 in tuition to attend 2,000 hours of school—never mind the fact that most of the schools in Utah didn't teach the hair braiding she was doing.

Jestina appealed to a government board comprised largely of licensed cosmetologists—the gatekeepers of the profession's licensure scheme—and was denied. She sued the state and won, but the case cost taxpayers around $200,000 in legal fees. The judge in her case opined, "The right to work for a living in the common occupations of the community is of the very essence of the personal freedom and opportunity that the Constitution was designed to protect."[63] It was a huge victory for an admittedly small issue, but cosmetologists were kicking and screaming throughout the entire process, objecting to any loosening of the licensure requirements and the accompanying increase in competition. Jealousy was also a factor; I spoke with numerous hair stylists who felt it unfair that she should "get off the hook" while they were made to jump through regulatory hurdles. This was echoed by a spokesman for the Professional Beauty

Association who asked, "Why should everyone else who's doing hair have to conform to requirements and not her?"[64] The testimony offered by cosmetologists to the legislature, in asking for continued regulation on their industry, was couched not in terms of economic protectionism (because then, of course, they would have exposed themselves) but in fearful terms of cosmetological calamities that might befall the citizenry should unregulated hair braiders be allowed to service the masses. Chemical burns, contamination, diseases—these and more were conjured up as doomsday scenarios for lawmakers and the public at large, should policies they disagreed with be enacted. Of course, these proponents of regulation didn't divulge the fact that even license-holding cosmetologists can and do introduce disease, burn their clients, or otherwise cause problems. The narrative of fear was reinforced, as it is with most circumstances in which economic protectionism is present, thus generating support for proposed policies that will allegedly ensure the safety, health, and welfare of the public.

We see the same unbalanced representation in a variety of industries. The nightly news doesn't report that "millions of gun owners around the country carried their firearms all day today, and nobody got hurt!" This story is uncontroversial, and thus unreported. Instead, only the extremely infrequent atrocities are presented, suggesting that the threat is larger than it actually is. Journalists don't remind the public that nearly 100,000 successful and safe airplane flights occur each day in the skies above the United States of America, but they do highlight the problems when they occur. Food poisoning elicits mass panic and recalls of millions of items. An act of apparent terrorism receives wall-to-wall coverage, inundating viewers with talking points and propaganda. Each new event instills fear, but the fear is so effective because it almost always lacks context. One's mind does not usually consider, in a moment of crisis, that a perceived threat might be overblown, misrepresented, or extremely infrequent.

Rather, the usual response consists of a call for somebody to "do something" about it.

In response to crisis, we demand action. We want to ensure that the threat we see before us is neutralized and that all future threats are averted. Having experienced a home invasion, for example, the victimized family might be prompted to obtain a firearm or install alarms. Scary spiders terrorizing a nervous mother would likely lead to a visit from a pest control company. This same reactionary response applies to public policy; fearing unemployment, the American laborer whose job is being undermined by a Chinese immigrant— or a Mexican one, or a teenager—often expects, and demands, legal protection to shield him from competition. A hijacked plane is used as a weapon, and the public lines up in support of warrantless searches and seizures, invasive pat downs, and other restrictions. People desire calm, and this is what savvy despots claim to offer. In pursuit of tranquility, and being afraid of fear, people abdicate their liberty.

NOTES

1. Radhey Shyam Chaurasi, *History of Western Thought* (New Dehli: Atlantic Publishers, 2001), 308.
2. Theodore Dwight, ed., *History of the Hartford Convention* (New York: N. & J. White, 1833).
3. Andrew Napolitano, *A Nation of Sheep* (Nashville: Thomas Nelson, 2007), 7.
4. Michael Kent Curtis, *Free Speech, the People's Darling Privilege* (Durham: Duke University Press, 2000).
5. Ibid.
6. "The Sentence of Vallandigham," *The New York Times*, May 21, 1863.
7. "Gov. Seymour's Letter," *The New York Times*, May 19, 1863.
8. John G. Nicolay and John Hay, eds., *Abraham Lincoln: Complete Works, Comprising His Speeches, Letters, State Papers and Miscellaneous Writings, vol. 2* (The Century Co., 1894).
9. Joseph Hartwell Barrett, *Life of Abraham Lincoln* (New York: Moore, Wilstach & Baldwin, 1865), 295.
10. J. Russell Young, "Roosevelt Explains Social Aims at Press Conference," *Washington Star*, June 10, 1935.
11. Congressional Record, May 27, 1935.
12. "FDR's Statements on Social Security," Social Security Administration, accessed August 2, 2014, http://www.ssa.gov/history/fdrstmts.html#signing.
13. William C. Rives, ed., *History of the Life and Times of James Madison, vol. 1* (Boston: Little, Brown, 1859), 636.
14. "Rumsfeld: It Would Be A Short War," CBS News, November 15, 2002, accessed August 2, 2014, http://www.cbsnews.com/news/rumsfeld-it-would-be-a-short-war/.
15. F.A. Hayek, *The Road to Serfdom: Text and Documents—The Definitive Edition* (Routledge: The University of Chicago Press, 2007), 156.

16. "Balancing Act: National Security and Civil Liberties in Post-9/11 Era," Pew Research Center, June 7, 2013, accessed August 2, 2014, http://www.pewresearch.org/fact-tank/2013/06/07/balancing-act-national-security-and-civil-liberties-in-post-911-era/.

17. "Poll Finds Strong Acceptance for Public Surveillance," *The New York Times*, April 30, 2013, accessed August 2, 2014, http://www.nytimes.com/2013/05/01/us/poll-finds-strong-acceptance-for-public-surveillance.html.

18. "Susie Castillo Assaulted by TSA ," YouTube, April 26, 2011, accessed August 2, 2014, https://www.youtube.com/watch?v=14mKoAptaiw.

19. Milton Mayer, *They Thought They Were Free: The Germans, 1933-45* (Chicago: The University of Chicago Press, 1966), xvii-xix.

20. Ibid, 255.

21. Ibid, xix.

22. Ibid, 167.

23. "The Good Germans: Inside the Resistance to the Nazis," Foreign Affairs, accessed August 2, 2014, http://www.foreignaffairs.com/articles/141489/peter-hoffmann/the-good-germans.

24. *They Thought They Were Free*, 169-172.

25. Stanley Milgram, *Obedience to Authority: An Experimental View* (New York: Harper Perennial, 1983), xii.

26. "Violent unrest breaks out in Tunisian capital," *Reuters*, January 11, 2011, accessed August 2, 2014, http://www.reuters.com/article/2011/01/11/us-tunisia-protests-idUSTRE70A2GO20110111.

27. James Boswell, *Life of Johnson* (Oxford: OUP, 1989) 477.

28. Johann Wolfgang von Goethe, *Goethe's Opinions* (London: John W. Parker and Son, 1853), 3.

29. Edward Bernays, *Propaganda* (Brooklyn: Ig Publishing, 2005), 47.

30. Scott M. Cutlip, *The Unseen Power: Public Relations: A History* (Hillsdale: Lawrence Earlbaum Associates, Inc., 1994), 185.

31. *Propaganda*, 37-38.

32. *The Century of Self*, directed by Adam Curtis (2002).

33. *Propaganda*, 48.

34. "Nazi Propaganda," Holocaust Encyclopedia, accessed August 2, 2014, http://www.ushmm.org/wlc/en/article.php?ModuleId=10005202.

35. Edward Bernays, *Biography of an Idea: Memoirs of Public Relations Counsel* (New York: Simon & Schuster, 1965), 652.

36. Oliver Thomson, *Mass Persuasion in History: An Historical Analysis of the Development of Propaganda Techniques* (Crane, Russak & Co., 1977), 111.

37. "Catapult the Propaganda," YouTube, accessed August 2, 2014, https://www.youtube.com/watch?v=VxnegxNEDAc.

38. Michael Parenti, *Dirty Truths: Reflections on Politics, Media, Ideology, Conspiracy, Ethnic Life, and Class Power* (San Francisco: City Lights Books, 1996), 57.

39. David O. McKay, Conference Report, April 1951, 92-98.

40. John R. Lott, Jr., *The Bias Against Guns* (Washington, DC: Regnery Publishing, 2003), 40.

41. David L. Altheide and R. Sam Michalowski, "Fear in the News: A Discourse of Control," Arizona State University, accessed August 2, 2014, http://www.public.asu.edu/~atdla/fearinthenews.pdf.

42. Ibid.

43. David L. Altheide, "Notes Towards A Politics Of Fear," *Journal for Crime, Conflict and the Media (1)*, 37-54.

44. "The 'prop-agenda' war," *Asia Times*, July 2, 2004, accessed August 2, 2014, http://www.atimes.com/atimes/Front_Page/FG02Aa02.html.

45. "Putin talks NSA, Syria, Iran, drones in RT interview," Russia Today, June 12, 2013, accessed August 2, 2014, http://rt.com/news/putin-rt-interview-full-577/.

46. Sara Firth, Twitter post, July 18, 2014, https://twitter.com/Sara__Firth/statuses/490070995831910401.

47. "Russia Today Correspondent Resigns Over Coverage Of Ukrainian Plane Crash," Buzzfeed, July 18, 2014, accessed August 2, 2014, http://www.buzzfeed.com/jimwaterson/russia-today-correspondent-resigns-over-coverage-of-ukranian.

48. "A Brief History of the Smith-Mundt Act and Why Changing It Matters," MountainRunner.us, accessed August 2, 2014, http://mountainrunner.us/2012/02/history_of_smith-mundt/.

49. "U.S. Repeals Propaganda Ban, Spreads Government-Made News to Americans," Foreign Policy, July 14, 2013, accessed August 2, 2014, http://thecable.foreignpolicy.com/posts/2013/07/12/us_backs_off_propaganda_ban_spreads_government_made_news_to_americans.

50. "A few words of praise for some of the reporters covering Israeli-Palestinian violence," *The Baltimore Sun*, July 17, 2014, accessed July 18, 2014, http://www.baltimoresun.com/entertainment/tv/z-on-tv-blog/bal-tv-reporters-gaza-israel-warfare-20140716,0,5445863.story.

51. Ayman Mohyeldin, Twitter post, July 16, 2014, https://twitter.com/AymanM/statuses/489417783814258689.

52. "CNN boots reporter from Israel-Gaza conflict after 'scum' tweet," Russia Today, July 18, 2014, accessed August 2, 2014, http://rt.com/usa/173888-cnn-reporter-scum-israel/.

53. "MSNBC Contributor Accuses Network Of 'Biased' Coverage Toward Israel," *The Huffington Post*, July 21, 2014, accessed July 22, 2014, http://www.huffingtonpost.com/2014/07/21/rula-jebreal-msnbc-palestinians-airtime_n_5606673.html.

54. "Journalist Who Accused MSNBC Of Pro-Israel Bias: I've Been Canceled!," Talking Points Memo, July 23, 2014, accessed July 23, 2014, http://talkingpointsmemo.com/livewire/rula-jebreal-israel-msnbc-canceled.

55. "'Witch Hunt': Fired MSNBC Contributor Speaks Out on Suppression of Israel-Palestine Debate," AlterNet, July 23, 2014, accessed July 23, 2014, accessed http://www.alternet.org/media/witch-hunt-fired-msnbc-contributor-speaks-out-networks-witch-hunt-and-suppression-israel.

56. Ibid.

57. "Lights, Camera… Covert Action: The Deep Politics of Hollywood," GlobalResearch, January 21, 2009, accessed August 2, 2014.

58. "Valerie Jarrett to Hollywood: Shill for Obamacare in Your Scripts," Breitbart, March 28, 2014, accessed August 2, 2014.

59. "US military studied how to influence Twitter users in Darpa-funded research," *The Guardian*, July 8, 2014, accessed July 12, 2014, http://www.theguardian.com/world/2014/jul/08/darpa-social-networks-research-twitter-influence-studies.

60. Ibid.

61. The Chinese Exclusion Act of 1882 was the first federal legislation restricting immigration.

62. "So You Think You Can Be a Hair Braider?," New York Times, June 12, 2012, accessed August 2, 2014, http://www.nytimes.com/2012/06/17/magazine/so-you-think-you-can-be-a-hair-braider.html.

63. "Federal Judge Strikes Down Utah's Hairbraiding License Requirements," Libertas Institute, August 9, 2012, accessed August 2, 2014, http://libertasutah.org/blog/breaking-federal-judge-strikes-down-utahs-hairbraiding-license-requirements/.

64. "So You Think…," *The New York Times*.

THE TEMPESTUOUS SEA OF LIBERTY

"The sea is dangerous and its storms terrible, but these obstacles have never been sufficient reason to remain ashore. Unlike the mediocre, intrepid spirits seek victory over those things that seem impossible. It is with an iron will that they embark on the most daring of all endeavors, to meet the shadowy future without fear and conquer the unknown."
—Attributed to Ferdinand Magellan

CAN YOU IMAGINE A LIFE without government providing some sort of material care or comfort? In an age now forgotten, Americans generally embraced a strong work ethic and a rugged independence, leading Alexis de Tocqueville to observe that the average person was "taught from his earliest infancy to rely on his own exertions in order to resist the evils and difficulties of life; he looks upon social authority with an eye of mistrust and anxiety and he only claims its assistance when he is quite unable to shift without it."[1] Contrast this historical observation against the present day: almost half of all Americans live in a household that receives some form of government aid.[2] Government officials in charge of supervising and reporting on these welfare programs do not even know how many there are.[3]

It is safe to say that many people would prefer to be taken care of "from cradle to grave" by the government. Consider the fictional "Julia," a character created by the Barack Obama 2012 re-election campaign to highlight how the president's policies "help one woman over her lifetime," implying the same sort of benefits for all Americans. This rather creepy campaign piece shows this cradle-to-grave application of government dependency, following Julia from age three to 67. At each phase of her life, she is shown thriving due only to taxpayer-funded, government-mandated programs: Head Start preschool, public education, college grants, taxpayer-backed student loans, mandatory health care plans, reproductive medical services, business subsidies, and welfare programs. It was, in the words of a critic, "a celebration of a how a woman can live her entire life by leaning on government intervention, dependency and other people's money rather than her own initiative or hard work."[4] The fact that a presidential campaign decided to produce this shows that a large number of Americans, likely numbering in the tens of millions at a minimum, want or expect government assistance throughout their lives. The fact that a president could successfully campaign by using such ads shows that the foundation of each of these government programs is fear: fear of uncertainty, lack of opportunity, and suffering. Each new mandate, created with the ostensible goal of promoting stability and calm, is a despotic act imposed upon those who dissent—people who would rather use their own money to secure their own independence, stabilize their own future, and pursue their own happiness.

Having looked at the calm of despotism, we now turn our attention to its antithesis, which Jefferson described as "tempestuous," or in other documented sources as "boisterous." As both an ardent student of history and an active participant in the events surrounding the American Revolution, Jefferson was not using a rhetorical flourish when he wrote about the "tempestuous sea of liberty." He recognized that liberty was not utopia, and that it required education, integrity, and vigor. Jefferson also observed that this sea "is never without a wave,"[5] suggesting that liberty does not guarantee calm. Put differently, liberty effectively brings with it some amount of turbulence.

Let's first look at the effect of unemployment on instability. An individual hired to perform a task is dependent upon the employer for a steady paycheck. Forces outside his control affect the employer's ability to continue his employment; loss of clients, a faulty investment, or tightened banking regulations, among many other factors, might affect the employer's bottom line. Through no fault of his own, the worker may find himself out of a job, compelled to look elsewhere to provide for his family. Absent a "social safety net" comprised of a myriad of opportunities to be taken care of by taxpayers, the individual would be incentivized to look expeditiously for new work or perhaps work for less pay than he might have hoped. Perhaps, due to economic circumstances such as a depression, it would be extremely difficult to find anybody willing to hire him. These financial ups and downs, which bring with them stress, familial strife, and other negative effects, are clearly tumultuous.

But unemployment isn't the fundamental issue here—what truly bothers people, and what induces a feeling of fear, is uncertainty. Imagine if our fictional friend had a significant amount of savings set aside for circumstances such as his unexpected job loss. He would not fear, because he had prepared. As a result of his stabilized circumstances, he would not be uncertain about where to find the next meal or if he could keep his home. On the other hand, an individual who was entirely dependent upon his paycheck to provide for himself and his family would find himself seeking dependence on some new source—and that's where the government swoops in to continue that dependence and provide for economic "calm." Many people prefer not only to be provided for, but *planned* for—if they can't or won't think of their future, they expect somebody else to. Uncertainty becomes a phobia from which people hope to flee, despite its being, as Stephen R. Covey once wrote, the "one thing that's certain about life."[6]

Those seeking calm not only want to be planned for themselves, at least to some degree—they also want *others* planned for as well. They fear the actions of their peers, and the effect it may have on them. They want their neighbors to keep their lawns weed-free and their fences painted a certain color, so they organize a Homeowners Association to impose that majoritarian mandate on those who dissent. They want to be sure they never encounter a safety threat, so they support suspicionless searches, seizures, and pat downs. They use prescription medication or other substances responsibly but don't trust others to do the same, so they support restrictions, taxes, and regulation to discourage abuse. They know they have nothing to hide, but they're not sure about that guy down the street, so they support warrantless wiretapping and mass surveillance. In short, they fear the tempestuous sea of liberty not because they don't know how to navigate it themselves, but because they worry that others might ram and sink their ship. Imagine how a typical New York City resident would feel seeing a man walk down the street with a handgun on his hip. Of course, the city has made it illegal to do so precisely because of the reaction you just envisioned. People are uncomfortable not being able to predict what others will do.

The American experiment was an attempt to learn from past republics and can be seen as an effort to build a better, stronger ship to navigate the sea of liberty with more success than past societies had done. (Whether that ship remains afloat today is a subject worth pondering.) Twenty-nine years after winning their independence, in a July 4th celebration held in Boston—one of the focal points of the American Revolution—townspeople gathered to hear an oration in honor of their collective liberation from their mother country. Aaron Hall Putnam, a member of Thomas Jefferson's Democratic-Republican party, highlighted the trend of nations to degrade from freedom to dependence:

> The history of republics, in all ages, presents to us the same spectacle. We trace the same effects resulting from similar causes. In most instances, having by a bloody and arduous revolutionary struggle, liberated themselves from the chains of despotism. We then behold them, "in the full tide of experiment," with impetuous career, launch forth into the "tempestuous sea of liberty." We see them, tossing upon its wild waves, dashing against its hidden rocks, driven by the furious currents of faction in every direction; and at length, after struggling through scenes of confusion and horror, we leave them again, weary, weather beaten and indifferent to their fate, in the sullen, silent, dreary "calm of despotism." This is not exaggeration, not merely the language of declamation— it is reality, what has happened and probably always will happen. To realize this description, let us hastily survey the monumental ruins of ancient republics of whom we can only say, they once flourished; now, they are no more.
>
> What mighty power subverted the famous republics of Greece, united in a federal compact similar to our own; renowned for the wisdom of their sages, the patriotic valor of their citizens, and their ardent love of liberty? How fell the commercial republic of Carthage, opulent and powerful in resources? The mighty Roman republic, at whose name the whole world trembled, celebrated for her patriots, heroes, and statesmen? They were subverted by the furious convulsions of popular licentiousness. Artful and ambitious men, flattering the vanities and vices

of the multitude, inflaming their passions against the established government, rose on the storm of popular frenzy to supreme power, and enslaved the people whom they had deluded with the "siren song" of liberty and equal rights.

The same delusive arts, which enabled the parricides of ancient liberty, to overthrow these illustrious republics of old, have uniformly been adopted by the demagogues and false patriots of modern times.[7]

What Putnam was getting at was the fact that no ship has ever successfully navigated the sea of liberty for very long. Many would prefer to stay on the shores, protected from seasickness and stormy waves. They desire liberty without its responsibilities, and therefore seek a middle ground in which they can enjoy a semblance of freedom while having a safety net upon which to rely when the going gets rough. They are like their forebears of whom Alexis de Tocqueville remarked were "constantly excited by two conflicting passions: they want to be led, and they wish to remain free." This trend, he said, results in the very historical outcome which Putnam observed; as people desire planning for their lives and others, to produce stability and comfort, the government "covers the surface of society with a network of small complicated rules, minute and uniform, through which the most original minds and the most energetic characters cannot penetrate, to rise above the crowd." De Tocqueville continued:

The will of man is not shattered, but softened, bent, and guided; men are seldom forced by it to act, but they are constantly restrained from acting. Such a power does not destroy, but it prevents existence; it does not tyrannize, but it compresses, enervates, extinguishes, and stupefies a people, till each nation is reduced to nothing better than a flock of timid and industrious animals, of which the government is the shepherd.[8]

While many desire the calm of despotism, there are those who are willing to accept the risks inherent in a life of liberty. Doing so requires contextualizing and overcoming the fears that quite literally saturate our lives. In hopes of security, and succumbing to the deceptions and propaganda of politicians and pundits, people are surrendering the very thing that makes life worth living at all—their liberty. As Supreme Court Justice Robert Jackson once wrote, "Implicit in the term 'national defense' is the notion of defending those values and ideas which set this nation apart… It would be ironic if, in the name of national defense, we would sanction the subversion of… those liberties… which make the defense of the nation worthwhile."[9] Fear has crippled the citizenry, paralyzed otherwise patriotic people, and produced a "flock of timid and industrious animals" spooked by each subsequent hobgoblin presented to them. Those concerned with this trend must identify it and implement ways to correct it.

EMBRACING TRUTH

"We need not be ignorant of real threats to our safety," wrote former Congressman Ron Paul, "against which we must remain vigilant. We need only to banish to the ash heap of history the notion that we ought to be ruled by our fears and those who use them to enhance their own power."[10] That latter point is worth emphasizing: in addition to changing our own reactions to fearful circumstances, it's especially important that we withdraw support from those who are clearly encouraging and exploiting them. Experiencing fear does not necessarily lead to objectionable consequences—for example, you can be afraid of thunder without doing anything you'd regret afterward—but when fear is coupled with a recommendation from someone who stands to gain from our fears, it can lead to ruin. Thus, it is imperative that those who operate on fear—which, frankly, can be all of us—ensure that the recommendations they're acting on, and the policies they are supporting, come from trustworthy sources.

In a world of people "crying wolf" for their own gain, be they corporate executives, politicians, media outlets, or others, those who value liberty are compelled to wade through the sticky muck of opinions and suggestions to find the truth. It's like Leo Tolstoy said: "The truth is obtained like gold: not by letting it grow bigger, but by washing off from it everything that isn't gold."[11] In our world, this means first recognizing that traditional media outlets have been compromised. This isn't exactly revelatory; many journalists have sounded this same warning for years. "We lie about everything—lying has become the staple," said investigative journalist Seymour Hersh, who suggested that journalism could be fixed by closing down the main media outlets and firing 90% of editors.[12] "Our house is on fire… We're getting the big stories wrong, over and over again," admitted Scott Pelley, managing editor at CBS.[13] Worse than conveying inaccuracies as truth is the unwillingness to challenge the propaganda; journalism is, ideally, the attempt to "afflict the comfortable" by investigating the claims made by those in power.

In many ways, truth has become difficult to uncover because those who attempt to do so are attacked not only by those in power, but by those whose job it theoretically is to be "washing off" the muck. In response to the Edward Snowden leaks and Glenn Greenwald's reporting of them, many journalists have turned their ire toward Greenwald and his associates for airing the government's dirty laundry in public. Decisions regarding which government secrets to publicize, said one journalist, "must ultimately be made by the government."[14] Jeffrey Toobin, a legal analyst for CNN, argued that Snowden shouldn't have given the documents to the press (even though his own station reported on them) but that he should have gone "to an inspector general, to Congress, he can work through the established channels"[15]—never mind the fact that those "channels" are designed to suppress, excuse away, and justify the corruption.

When lying becomes mainstream, it's a good idea to seek out those who challenge the narrative. They can often be identified, as in Greenwald's case, when they're being attacked by the establishment. It's important to recall in this story why Greenwald is even relevant. When asked to explain why he chose this blogger-turned-journalist to publish the leaked documents, Snowden pointed to his history:

> The bottom line is that sources risking serious harm to return public information to public hands must have absolute confidence that the journalists they go to will report on that information rather than bury it. Glenn's writing consistently demonstrated his belief that journalists should serve people rather than governments, and that gives sources the confidence to shoulder great risks to do good.[16]

Just as the boy who cried wolf developed a clearly problematic track record, we should identify and support those who have a consistent and truthful track record. While anybody can make mistakes—we shouldn't necessarily expect journalistic perfection—it becomes evident when the supposed truth-tellers are repeatedly anything but. There's a reason why only 6% of Americans rate the news media as "very trustworthy."[17] Going against the "mainstream" narrative, as in Greenwald's case, can often be an indicator of independence and a sincere interest in the truth. Independence is itself an important factor in truth-telling. Reporters working for a media outlet with strong ties to the establishment may be persuaded to suppress the truth to some degree, since they have an interest in not challenging those in power, for fear of losing access, among other things. Robert W. McChesney, a prolific communications professor whose work focuses on the role of media in society, explains:

> To maintain neutrality, journalists are loath to call out one side for lying. They also do not want to antagonize their sources, upon whom they are dependent. Instead,

journalists prefer to report that one side is calling the other side liars and leave it at that. We report; you decide. The problem is that the liars can dismiss the criticism as being driven by their opponents and ignore it, so this becomes a liar's paradise.[18]

Of course, the "side" most quoted is that of the propagandists— those with the power, promise of access, and money to ensure their message becomes the adopted societal narrative. For this reason, political and journalistic decentralization are both important. Diffusing power to local levels, and encouraging investigation by the masses and not by the few, offers the greatest chance at determining and defending the truth. Fear is less potent in smaller quantities— when widely poured across an entire society, it is more likely to be successfully weaponized.

What each individual first needs is confidence that they can determine and understand the truth. Prior to the invention of the printing press by Johannes Gutenberg in 1436, it was economically unfeasible for most individuals to own books, as they required costly transcription by scribes. As a result, most people were only functionally literate, if that. Without the ability to read information, let alone scrutinize and judge it, commoners had no intellectual defense with which they could combat falsehoods. The printing revolution empowered people to access and act upon truth, thus holding people accountable for their misdeeds: corrupt religious leaders acting in defiance of the Bible, corrupt politicians violating the law, etc. Technology continues to revolutionize our access to truth. In our day, it combats the centralization of information by empowering each individual to be an investigative reporter and to share what they've discovered with the entire world. Glenn Greenwald, whose name is now known throughout the world for his truth-telling, started as a blogger. Matt Drudge, famous for his heavily trafficked Drudge Report website, got started using an email list sent to a few friends. Each person is potentially a reporter, and while this can create confusion—the internet is certainly known for being littered with wild theories and false claims—it also enables a broader distribution of coverage of any given topic. When more people are involved in investigating something, the chances of the truth remaining hidden decrease.

After Jesus Christ referenced his work in teaching the truth to others, Pontius Pilate replied, "What is truth?"[19] Like him, many believe that the truth either cannot be known, or is not worth the time, energy, and stress to discover. Others simply believe completely incorrect things, such as one out of every four Americans who evidently believe that the sun revolves around the Earth.[20] This prevalence of ignorance has a scientific basis as explained by two scientists in an opinion piece titled, "Your brain lies to you":

> The brain does not simply gather and stockpile information as a computer's hard drive does. Facts are stored first in the hippocampus, a structure deep in the brain about the size and shape of a fat man's curled pinkie finger. But the information does not rest there. Every time we recall it, our brain writes it down again, and during this re-storage, it is also reprocessed. In time, the fact is gradually transferred to the cerebral cortex and is separated from the context in which it was originally learned. For example, you know that the capital of California is Sacramento, but you probably don't remember how you learned it.[21]

This is known as source amnesia, and often leads people to forget whether a statement is true or false. For example, a statement that was initially qualified, or even presented as an outright lie, can eventually stand alone in the person's mind as being true. The article's authors note that this phenomenon can be used for political gain: "Even if they do not understand the neuroscience behind source amnesia, campaign strategists can exploit it to spread misinformation." Thus, the Bush administration was able to solicit support for intervention in Iraq because people had come to believe the earlier statements and inferences that Saddam was somehow responsible for 9/11.

While amnesia is a detriment to discovering truth, so too is our collectively short attention span. Media institutions profit off of successive, short stories. It's why we call them "sound bytes"— an entire "meal" of information would lead people to change the channel. Those who are led along this frenetic pace of information consumption lack the time or energy to dig deep into all of the issues and therefore do no research or fact checking at all to see if what they've been told is indeed correct. Few Americans remember that then-Secretary of Defense Donald Rumsfeld once announced, in a press conference, a military "matter of life and death." His concern was not foreign terrorists. "The adversary's closer to home," he said. "It's the Pentagon bureaucracy." Rumsfeld went on to explain that the Pentagon's own auditors disclosed that they could not account for some 25% of what was being spent. "According to some estimates we cannot track $2.3 trillion in transactions," Rumsfeld admitted.[22] That staggering sum should have sent shockwaves through the system, enraging tax-sensitive Americans, but it didn't. Why? The reason is that Rumsfeld's press conference was held on September 10, 2001. The next day, airplane hijackers attacked the Pentagon and the World Trade Center in New York City, captivating the world's attention; unrelated news was no longer newsworthy. This report of massive waste and corruption was sent down the Orwellian memory hole. Had Americans been reminded of this waste, they perhaps would not have stood by idly while political leaders bathed the Pentagon in a steady stream of new money for Middle Eastern interventions in the months and years that followed. Putting the event in the context of Rumsfeld's report, they might not have been so susceptible to fearmongering. Had they been aware of the truth, they perhaps would not have accepted the lies. For those who seek the truth in an effort to dispel the lies and fear that permeate society, context and recollection are key; recognizing the trustworthiness of a given source requires *remembering* and *recording*. We need to keep track of past claims, our research of them, and the sources from which they came.

Finally, embracing the truth requires setting aside partisan preferences and interfering loyalties. Even civil society has become divided in terms of warring countries, sparring sports teams, rival political parties, and other factions that create opposition between people. The "enemy" is suggested to be spouting lies and propaganda, while the domestic leaders are portrayed as near-demigods who can do no wrong and who only have the public's best interest in mind. Through propaganda and media control, any flaws of the "home team" and its leaders are minimized or suppressed, and their positive aspects are augmented or created out of whole cloth. Rejecting the propaganda and our fears of the "other side" may lead us to concede

that the enemy may have legitimate grievances and that "our side" may not always be in the right. Indeed, the "enemy" may be right, while one's own government is in the wrong. Casting aside the narrative of fear may lead to the realization that those promoting it are the liars, twisting the truth enough to be beneficial to their purposes, while still assuming the appearance of truth so as to attract or pacify the unsuspecting masses.

Many people live in a Matrix-like deception regarding the world around them and are kept content by the perception of stability and happiness—smooth sailing across calm waters. When one awakens from that dream to find himself on board a tiny vessel on a tempestuous sea, he immediately experiences discomfort and uncertainty. Realizing that the foreign hegemony of the federal government might have more to do with oil and enterprise than with "spreading democracy" and liberating oppressed people is a hard punch in the gut for whose who have long been patriotically waving their flags, supporting the wars, and voting for the politicians who champion them. Watching friends and family give their lives in military service during a conflict purposefully ignited by a "false flag" incident can be enraging. The satisfaction of electing a political candidate on promises of transparency, tax reform, or other policy improvements soon gives way to the sad and common reality that such promises were nothing more than lies designed by professionals to excite a base of supporters to get out the vote.

These and other harsh realities are often ignored. They're raw, they're uncomfortable, and they require admitting at least some amount of blame on our part, if for nothing else than that we believed in the lie to begin with. In other cases, we may have participated in or perpetuated the lie, and embracing the truth then requires a recognition of more direct fault. But liberty demands that we pursue truth, even if it's difficult, in order to reduce our exposure to those who would exploit the lie to wield power over us. We must abandon tribalistic notions of "we are right, they are wrong," accepting the fact that we may be associating with folks who are liars, deceivers, robbers, betrayers, or even murderers. "Truth is treason in an empire of lies," as the saying goes, for this very reason: not only will those in power come after you, but so will the masses of individuals—your family, your coworkers, your peers—who have some sort of stake in the status quo. In psychology, this is known as system justification and involves one's defense of a system with which one is affiliated despite its corruption or injustice. "You have to understand," Morpheus explained to Neo in *The Matrix*, "most of these people are not ready to be unplugged. And many of them are so inured, so hopelessly dependent on the system, that they will fight to protect it." In contrast to this, those who desire a life of liberty, free from fear, should pattern themselves after Patrick Henry who observed:

> We are apt to shut our eyes against a painful truth... Is this the part of wise men, engaged in a great and arduous struggle for liberty? Are we disposed to be of the number of those who, having eyes, see not, and having ears, hear not...? For my part, whatever anguish of spirit it may cost, I am willing to know the whole truth.[23]

ASSUMING RISK

"A ship in harbor is safe," wrote the American author John Shed, "but that is not what ships are built for." As has been discussed in this book, national security and personal safety are often cited as reasons for which despotic policies are deemed necessary; in times of danger, liberty becomes of secondary importance to many who live in fear of attack. Pursuing liberty, however, does not mean acting in reckless fashion with no concern for one's safety. If anything, it merely means considering liberty to be an ideal and contextualizing dangers—seeing risk for what it truly is, and not what it's suggested to be by others who don't have our best interests (including our liberty) at heart. It also means rejecting policies that would violate liberty when the problems they purport to address are comparatively insignificant, as was explained by a political commentator for the *National Review*:

> We have suffered several thousand casualties from 9/11 through today. Suppose we had a 9/11-level attack with 3,000 casualties per year every year. Each person reading this would face a probability of death from this source of about 0.001% each year. A Republic demands courage—not foolhardy and unsustainable "principle at all costs," but reasoned courage—from its citizens. The American response should be to find some other solution to this problem if the casualty rate is unacceptable. To demand that the government "keep us safe" by doing things out of our sight that we have refused to do in much more serious situations so that we can avoid such a risk is weak and pathetic. It is the demand of spoiled children, or the cosseted residents of the imperial city.[24]

Bruce Fein, a constitutional lawyer who worked at the Department of Justice during the Reagan administration, affirmed the same sentiment at a debate regarding Edward Snowden. Discussing the flawed implementation of the "national security" tactics used by the government, especially in the post-9/11 era, Fein said:

> In 2012, there was a 68-year-old grandmother picking vegetables who was vaporized by a Predator drone based on the reliability of intelligence gathered by the NSA and the CIA. And she was killed with her 9-year-old granddaughter watching, who came to Washington, D.C., to testify about exactly what happened.

> She said yes, she was there, she had been asked to pick the vegetables by her grandmother, then it became very dark, and there were sounds overhead, from the

drone. Then she heard screaming. She couldn't tell where from. She thought it was her grandmother but she wasn't certain. Then she began to run. She was frightened to death. Then she looked at her hands and they were all bloody. She tried to stop the bleeding and couldn't. Her grandmother was dead.

That's the United States of America, at least in one instance. That's our government that did that, with authorities that are knowing and open, that we accept. That seems to me, however, not what we want to be as a government. It means that if we want to avoid being complicit in injustice, we need to accept risk, knowingly, because that's what civilized people do. You can't live in a country with liberty without taking risk. Get out of bed in the morning and you take risks. You want to reduce risk to zero? Put everybody in prison or kill them all. Then you have zero risk, right? And I submit, ladies and gentlemen, this is a very profound view of life that separates civilized from savage nations. You've gotta take risks. Not stupid ones. But you've got to remember that life is uncertain. And you want to make certain that you don't become complicit in injustice yourself. That reduces us to the opposition.[25]

Fein is right: liberty requires risk, and only a fully totalitarian society could remove all risk—and only by completely denying any amount of freedom. Removing the risk children face would require wrapping them in bubble wrap and locking them in their rooms. Removing the risk adults face would similarly require everybody be confined to padded rooms and denied access to any implements that could be used to harm themselves or another person. Of course, we laugh at and reject this dystopian description of a "safe society," and most people feel that some sort of balance is needed between security and liberty. This balance implies the "social safety net" described earlier, such that some amount of risk is reduced and individuals are shielded to a certain degree from their own decisions as well as life's uninvited circumstances. But liberty—true liberty—recognizes and accepts risk, while acting in a smart and sensible fashion to reduce it while preserving liberty.

One issue not yet discussed, though highly relevant to the question of safety versus liberty, is that of food. Over the years, there have been a number of foodborne illness outbreaks, including listeriosis on cantaloupes, killing 30 people; salmonella on eggs, causing 2,000 illnesses and a recall of 500 million eggs; salmonellosis in peanut butter, leading to over 20,000 cases of sickness and several deaths; and hepatitis A, infecting over 600 people, due to tainted green onions. Dozens of other recent outbreaks have occurred. These instances prompt local health boards, county inspectors, state regulatory agencies, and federal bureaucracies to intervene, inspect, and micro-manage the production, distribution, and sale of food items. This over-protective tendency even leads the government to prohibit informed people from taking risks the government deems unacceptable, such as consuming raw milk.

Citing a "public health duty" and "statutory directive,"[26] armed agents with the Food and Drug Administration, along with other law enforcement officials, raided a Pennsylvanian Amish community in 2011 in search of raw milk products which were being sold in a co-op to highly informed, willing and consenting customers. SWAT police raids have occurred on other facilities, including Rawesome Foods, also in 2011, on allegations that "unpasteurized dairy products were sold illegally and did not meet health standards." One news article notes that "Government regulators contend such products can be dangerous; there is scientific evidence linking disease outbreaks to raw milk. The milk can transmit bacteria, which can result in diarrhea, dangerously high fevers and in some cases death."[27] But we use or consume all sorts of products that, in excess or on their own, can cause health problems—think of tobacco, alcohol, over-the-counter drugs, household cleaners, etc. Further, as is the case with other overreactions to statistically insignificant threats, raw milk's potential for harm is low. From 2000 to 2007 there were 37 outbreaks and 800 illnesses. With an estimated 9.4 million American consumers of raw milk as of 2007, a person's risk of illness (*not* death) from drinking unpasteurized milk was 1 in 94,000 during that period[28]— close to the same risk of death by skydiving, half the risk of death by playing American football, and a third of the risk of death by scuba diving.[29] Highlighting one of the real reasons behind such aggressive enforcement of raw milk laws, a reporter observed, "Raw milk, in particular, has drawn regulatory scrutiny, largely because the politically powerful dairy industry has pressed the government to act." There, we caught a glimpse of truth amid the swirl of lies and deceptions. It's not so much about safety as it is forcing the competition into the regulatory shadows.

Joel Salatin, an outspoken farmer who has faced his own battles with regulatory agencies, is the author of several books including *Everything I Want to Do Is Illegal: War Stories from the Local Food Front*. Salatin offered this vision of liberty as it relates to food:

> Eliminate the USDA. Started by Abraham Lincoln to help farmers be successful, no government organization has ever so effectively destroyed its constituency. We now have twice as many prisoners as we have farmers. Every time the federal government manipulates a marketplace, it favors the largest players, subsidizes the status quo, and discourages innovation. I can think of no role whatsoever for the government to play in farming. From crop insurance to environmental protections, the result has been… increasing pharmaceutical and chemical dependency, genetically modified organisms, increasing food allergies and a nation that leads the world in the five

chronic non-infectious diseases. The USDA told us to eat margarine. It told us to eat hydrogenated oils. The famous food pyramid founded on carbohydrates like Twinkies and Pop Tarts directly accelerated the obesity and Type II diabetes epidemic. Indeed, we would be a far healthier nation had the government never told us what to eat.

The USDA food police tell us it's perfectly safe to feed your children Coca Cola, Cheerios, and pink slime, but it's unsafe to drink raw milk, eat compost-grown tomatoes or imbibe Aunt Matilda's home-made pickles. When the government gets between my lips and my throat, I consider that an invasion of privacy. Official orthodoxy equates sterile food with safe food, and yet our biology is not sterile. Research into tomatoes does not seek more nutrition or taste—it seeks harder orbs to withstand jostling for 2,000 miles in a tractor trailer. Hence, tasteless, nutritionless, cardboard tomatoes. I can think of nothing positive that the USDA has done that wouldn't occur better in the private sector, and I can think of many terrible atrocities and abuses we're currently suffering that would be less severe had the USDA not aided and abetted stewardship abuse. Yes, it is time to be angry about this.[30]

No system can exist that protects us from the risk of bad choices while preserving the freedom to make good ones. The two cannot co-exist; freedom requires risk. The pursuit of happiness entails leaving the harbor. We desire connections with family and friends, so we risk the dangers inherent in transportation as we drive and fly. We seek a more comfortable financial situation, so we risk failure, rejection, physical hazards, moral temptations, and other dangers as we navigate commerce and develop business opportunities. We want to leverage our time, so instead of cooking every meal ourselves we purchase food from the store or dine at a restaurant and thereby risk consuming an ingredient we shouldn't or getting sick. Risk is a part of everyday life, and those who live so fearfully that they want to be isolated from it end up supporting policies and actions that do not substantively diminish risk, but do diminish liberty. Acting on fear would lead a person to attempt constructing a sturdy ship to insulate him from the sea's tempests, even though doing so would require dismantling everybody else's ships for materials and supplies. Life is not necessarily enjoyable and wonderful just because risk is absent; in fact, taking the occasional risk could imbue life with meaning, gratitude, and wonder. "What we obtain too cheap," wrote Tom Paine, "we esteem too lightly; it is dearness only that gives everything its value."[31]

Putting potential risks in context, as previously discussed, requires data. Without information regarding how dangerous something is, we cannot adequately prepare and act. Reviewing death counts alone, it is clear that the common fears exploited by the government are actually quite rare, and yet the proposed policies to prevent them are comparatively costly, aggressive, and inimical to individual liberty. Since 9/11, the specter of terrorism has paralyzed people with fear and led to horrendous violations of our rights. What's worse, all of this has been done when the threat is extremely low. The U.S. Department of State noted that in the year 2011, 17 U.S. citizens were killed worldwide as a result of terrorism—a figure which includes deaths in Afghanistan, Iraq, and all other theaters of war. In contrast, the number of annual deaths from other causes are comparatively high. In the United States alone, 4,609 people were killed while working at their jobs during 2011; more than 6,000 people die each year by falling down, usually from a roof or ladder; HIV claimed the lives of 7,638 in 2011; 32,367 motor vehicle deaths occurred in that same year; excessive alcohol use kills approximately 80,000 people per year; obesity is a contributing factor in hundreds of thousands of deaths annually; and avoidable medical errors cause the deaths of between 100,000 and 200,000 people every year. A 2011 Report on Terrorism from the National Counterterrorism Center, on the other hand, notes that Americans are statistically just as likely to be "crushed to death by their televisions or furniture each year" as they are to be killed by a terrorist.[32] Put simply, we should not be persuaded to sacrifice any whit of our cherished liberty in an effort to prevent something that is so unlikely; our lives should not be governed by statistical improbabilities.

Liberty is not utopia; the sea, after all, is anything but calm. Freedom can be messy, and bad things may happen—financial insolvency, social instability, physical harm, or even death. But is life enjoyable when we are cowering in fear, safely inert? Or is it worth it to venture out into the world a little, weathering the storm of life to pursue some spectacular goals? "We can easily forgive a child who is afraid of the dark," as the proverb goes, but "the real tragedy of life is when men are afraid of the light."

ALL YOU NEED IS LOVE

What, then, is the antidote to fear? Information, context, and an accurate risk assessment are important as they help minimize fear—but they don't eliminate it. They might help us respond in a more rational fashion, but they do not displace fear and they are ineffective at helping us resolve others' fear. In this war of words, in which people seeking power and gain have turned fear into a highly successful weapon, what is our best defense? How can we inoculate ourselves and our loved ones against the effects of sustained attacks on our psyche, with fear-based propaganda permeating media, entertainment, news, education, culture, religion, and, frankly, nearly every facet of life?

Perhaps the lesson can be found in a popular children's film, *Monsters, Inc.* The plot of this movie is built around a common childhood fear of monsters, but more generally addresses the fear of the unknown or the "other guy." Monsters live in a city fueled by children's screams, which the monsters are trained to capture by sneaking into the children's bedrooms at night and scaring them. Ironically, the most effective monsters are actually terrified of the children they are scaring, having been warned by those in authority that the children are "toxic" and that a mere touch could potentially be fatal. Only when a young girl inadvertently enters the monster world does this fear-based narrative begin to unravel, enabling the monsters to see that the child is not the hobgoblin she has always been portrayed to be. As the monsters get to know the little girl, their hearts are changed, and they begin to see their frightening behavior from her point of view. The monsters realize that she is not dangerous, and that they could relate to and sympathize with her; she was no longer an "other." Eventually, the unstable, fear-based economy of Monstropolis was revealed and replaced by a more powerful and easily renewable fuel source: love and laughter.

While this film was produced prior to 9/11, its release date was about six weeks after the attacks. Clearly, its message—though ultimately unheeded—could not have been more timely. As fear began to saturate political discourse, business dealings, and personal conversations, people erected psychological barriers against entire nations of people, believing them to be uncivilized, cave-dwelling Arabs who hate freedom, virtue, and peace. Fear was the fuel that moved the machine forward, both domestically and internationally.

Love, on the other hand, could have presented a far different future. Love of those involved would have encouraged us to consider their grievances, perhaps realizing that the threat of terrorism was not conjured up out of thin air, but was instead a response to years of intervention by armed forces. Certainly any act of aggression should be repudiated, as in the case of the attacks on American soil on 9/11. But love would have offered sympathy to those whose loved ones died on that fateful day while also rejecting proposals to pursue and punish people not directly connected with the attack. Love definitely would have repudiated the displacement and deaths of hundreds of thousands of innocent people in pursuit of Middle Eastern hobgoblins. Love demands that we see others as we do ourselves: as people with passions, loyalties, family, goals, and rights.

Love does not require being naive as to true threats or the risks inherent in life. An abused wife must not submit to her husband even though she may love and forgive him. Love of others does not require pacifism, allowing others to dominate or destroy us. We must, of course, love ourselves and those around us enough to be willing to defend against an attack. But real love is self-sacrificing, as opposed to the selfishness of fear. When threatened with an attack, love leads us to look outside ourselves, sincerely caring about what might happen to others. While we want to be safe, we resist the urge to support whatever policy we're told will make that happen. We care about the consequences—and not merely the promises—of each proposed policy, recognizing that they may negatively impact others, intentionally or not. When love is a motivating factor in our thought pattern, we are willing to embrace risk and sacrifice our comfort, even our own life if necessary, if it will produce the greatest outcome for those we care about. "Greater love hath no man than this," said Jesus, "that a man lay down his life for his friends."[33]

When we love others—even those we don't personally know—we are more apt to empathize with their circumstances. We mourn with those who are malnourished, or who lack adequate medical care, or whose family member died in warfare. In short, we humanize others, thus rejecting the political propaganda that first requires dehumanizing an enemy as a condition of creating support for attacking that enemy. Love leads us to see others as part of a brotherhood of mankind, rather than part of a rival faction that we should oppose in order to support our own team. We become, through love, a living embodiment of the Golden Rule, treating others as we desire to be treated ourselves.

Of course, all of these fanciful scenarios are fundamentally at odds with the society we live in—so far afield from the status quo that they're quite difficult to conceive. This doesn't suggest that behaviors and policies based on love are untenable in modern society. Rather, it is merely an indictment of the extent to which we have become steeped in a culture of fear. Our question, however, was one of defense—how do we counteract this fear that is all around us? Love is the answer. Fortunately, it is infectious. The scales fell from the monsters' eyes quite quickly as they realized that children could be loved instead of feared. Their behavior changed, thus introducing the power of love and laughter to the many other monsters who had been conditioned to fear children. The same opportunity presents itself in our day to people like ourselves who have been conditioned our whole lives to fear the uncertainties of life, the unknown of the world around us, and the dehumanized "others."

On March 14, 2012, Ronny Edry posted a photo on Facebook of himself and his daughter, who was holding the Israeli flag. Edry, an Israeli graphic designer, overlaid the photo with some text that read: "Iranians: we will never bomb your country. We ♥ You." For months, Israeli politicians had openly discussed the idea of preemptively striking Iran to halt its nuclear program. Media coverage and public opinion were intense, and the fear of attack led many Israelis to support the proposal. Amid all the saber-rattling, Edry's social media campaign took on a life of its own, producing responses from Iranians who had seen and been impacted by the outreach. "You have to understand," Edry later commented, "in Israel, we don't talk to people from Iran. We don't know people from Iran."[34] They were, after all, "the enemy." One young Iranian woman sent Edry a message describing the impact his message of love had on her:

> I am crying now after seeing your page. For years they painted the Israeli flag on the floor of our school so upon entering the school we would walk over it. It

never worked. We never developed hated towards you, never! Still, every time I looked at the Israeli flag I got a bad feeling in my stomach that I did not like. After seeing your daughter holding the flag, I do not feel that way any more and I am so happy. Now, I love that blue, I love that star, I love that flag. I [would] love to have you visit my country, my home, and see how beautiful it is... We love you, too.[35]

Edry's campaign was organically copycatted by people around the world, most heavily in Middle Eastern countries, who began producing similar images targeted at individuals living in supposed "enemy" nations. "These are people who are supposed to be enemies, on the verge of a war," Edry said. "And suddenly, people on Facebook are starting to say 'I like this guy,' 'I love those guys.'" The spontaneous and highly successful effort to humanize one another brought with it significant attention from international media outlets. The result of all of this, in Edry's view? "We're showing respect one to another, and we're understanding." A narrative of fear had been counteracted, for some, by a campaign based on love.

Fear leads to despotism; love leads to liberty. Acting selflessly disarms those who weaponize fear, for if our concern for ourselves has decreased in relation to other considerations, such as the well-being of our friends and family, then conniving politicians cannot exploit our emotions as easily. Hobgoblins are exposed for the fiction they truly are. Threats are contextualized. Enemies become brothers and sisters. It's as William Hazlitt once said: "The love of liberty is the love of others; the love of power is the love of ourselves."[36] A person who prioritizes love for others is not content with focusing on his own welfare, but is eager to reach out to others and improve their lives. This is the vision of a civil, productive, and prosperous society. Monstropolis realized that life is better when fueled with love and laughter. It's time we learned the same lesson.

NOTES

1. Alexis de Tocqueville, *The Republic of the United States of America* (New York: A. S. Barnes & Co., 1855), 204.

2. "Nearly Half of U.S. Lives in Household Receiving Government Benefit," *The Wall Street Journal*, October 5, 2011, accessed August 2, 2014, http://blogs.wsj.com/economics/2011/10/05/nearly-half-of-households-receive-some-government-benefit/.

3. "Federal Government Cannot Identify How Many Government Welfare Programs exist, Much Less Whether They Are Working," The Carleson Center for Public Policy, accessed August 2, 2014, http://theccpp.org/2011/09/federal-government-cannot-identify-how-many-government-welfare-programs-exist-much-less-whether-they.html.

4. "Who the Hell is 'Julia,' and Why am I Paying for Her Whole Life?," Human Events, May 3, 2012, accessed August 2, 2014, http://humanevents.com/2012/05/03/who-the-hell-is-julia-and-why-am-i-paying-for-her-whole-life/.

5. H. A. Washington, ed., *The Writings of Thomas Jefferson* (New York: J. C. Riker, 1855), 194.

6. Stephen R. Covey, *Predictable Results in Unpredictable Times* (Salt Lake City: FranklinCovey, 2009), v.

7. Aaron Hall Putnam, An Oration Pronounced July 4, 1805 (Charlestown: Samuel Etheridge, 1805), 12-13.

8. Alexis de Tocqueville, *Democracy in America, vol. 2* (New York: J. & H.G. Langley, 1840), 339.

9. *United States v. Robel*, 1968.

10. "The Fear Factor," Antiwar.com, July 31, 2007, accessed August 2, 2014, http://antiwar.com/paul/?articleid=11373.

11. R. F. Christian, ed., *Tolstoy's Diaries, vol. 2* (London: Athlone Press, 1985), 512.

12. "Seymour Hersh on Obama, NSA and the 'pathetic' American media," *The Guardian*, September 27, 2013, accessed August 2, 2014,

http://www.theguardian.com/media/media-blog/2013/sep/27/seymour-hersh-obama-nsa-american-media.

13. "CBS Anchor: 'We Are Getting Big Stories Wrong, Over and Over Again'," The Weekly Standard, May 11, 2013, accessed August 2, 2014, http://www.weeklystandard.com/blogs/cbs-anchor-we-are-getting-big-stories-wrong-over-and-over-again_722331.html.

14. "Eyes Everywhere," *The New York Times*, June 8, 2014, accessed August 2, 2014, http://www.nytimes.com/2014/06/08/books/review/no-place-to-hide-by-glenn-greenwald.html.

15. "Greenwald, Toobin Battle over Snowden on CNN: Corrupt Pols Get Promoted, Leakers Get Indicted," Mediaite, accessed August 2, 2014, http://www.mediaite.com/tv/greenwald-toobin-battle-over-snowden-on-cnn-corrupt-pols-get-promoted-leakers-get-indicted/.

16. "Enemy of the State," Advocate.com, November 12, 2013, accessed August 2, 2014, http://www.advocate.com/print-issue/current-issue/2013/11/12/enemy-state.

17. "Only 6% Rate News Media As Very Trustworthy," Rasmussen Reports, February 28, 2013, accessed August 2, 2014.

18. "The Rise of Establishment Reporting," Fairness and Accuracy in Reporting, November 1, 2013, accessed August 2, 2014, http://fair.org/extra-online-articles/the-rise-of-establishment-reporting/.

19. John 18:38

20. "1 In 4 Americans Thinks The Sun Goes Around The Earth, Survey Says," NPR, February 14, 2014, accessed August 2, 2014, http://www.npr.org/blogs/thetwo-way/2014/02/14/277058739/1-in-4-americans-think-the-sun-goes-around-the-earth-survey-says.

21. "Your brain lies to you," The New York Times, June 29, 2008, accessed August 2, 2014, http://www.nytimes.com/2008/06/29/opinion/29iht-edwang.1.14069662.html.

22. "The War On Waste," CBS, January 29, 2002, accessed August 2, 2014, http://www.cbsnews.com/news/the-war-on-waste/.

23. Harlow Giles Unger, *Lion of Liberty: Patrick Henry and the Call to a New Nation* (Philadelphia: Da Capo Press, 2010), 280.

24. "Against Waterboarding," National Review Online, April 29, 2009, accessed August 2, 2014, http://www.nationalreview.com/ corner/181094/against-waterboarding/jim-manzi.

25. "'Liberty and Justice for All' Means Security Risks," The Atlantic, March 25, 2014, accessed August 2, 2014, http://www.theatlantic. com/politics/archive/2014/03/liberty-and-justice-for-all-means-security-risks/359510/.

26. "Food safety chief defends raw milk raids," SFGate, June 7, 2011, accessed August 2, 2014, http://blog.sfgate.com/ nov05election/2011/06/07/food-safety-chief-defends-raw-milk-raids/.

27. "3 arrested on raw-milk charges," *Los Angeles Times*, August 4, 2011, accessed August 2, 2014, http://articles.latimes.com/2011/aug/04/ business/la-fi-milk-raid-20110804.

28. "Raw Milk Reality: Is Raw Milk Dangerous?," ChrisKresser.com, accessed August 2, 2014, http://chriskresser.com/raw-milk-reality-is-raw-milk-dangerous.

29. "Mountain mortality: a review of deaths that occur during recreational activities in the mountains," *Postgraduate Medical Journal*, vol. 85, issue 1004.

30. "Following Christ as a Lunatic Grass Farmer: An Interview with Joel Salatin," Food Freedom USA, accessed August 2, 2014, http://www. foodfreedomusa.org/food-freedom-usa-press/category/joel-salatin.

31. W. T. Sherwin, *Memoirs of the Life of Thomas Paine* (London: R. Carlile, 1819), 46.

32. "You're More Likely to Die from Brain-Eating Parasites, Alcoholism, Obesity, Medical Errors, Risky Sexual Behavior or Just About Anything OTHER THAN Terrorism," Washington's Blog, April 28, 2013, accessed August 2, 2014, http://www.washingtonsblog.com/2013/04/ statistics-you-are-not-going-to-be-killed-by-terrorists.html.

33. John 15:13

34. "Israel and Iran: A Love Story?" TED, December 21, 2012, accessed August 2, 2014, https://www.youtube.com/watch?v=6Lp-NMaU0r8.

35. Ibid.

36. William Hazlitt, *Political Essays, With Sketches of Public Characters* (London: William Hone, 1819), 168.

CONCLUSION

"Where the people fear the government you have tyranny.
Where the government fears the people you have liberty."[1]
—John Basil Barnhill

IN A POLL CONDUCTED IN April 2014, 37% of likely U.S. voters indicated that they fear the federal government. This high number can perhaps be attributed to the fact that 54% "consider the federal government today a threat to individual liberty rather than a protector."[2] If Barnhill is to be believed, we now live in an era in which tyranny, or despotism, is encroaching ever more forcefully. While modern America has so far been spared much of the fate of despotic regimes throughout history, including eugenics, slavery, suppression of free speech, martial law, and many other similarly punitive policies, decades of timidity have led us into "calm" despotism. Chains and whips are absent in commerce, but high taxation is itself a form of enslavement. We aren't usually incarcerated for free speech, but we can certainly be put on a TSA "no fly" list or made the subject of an IRS audit if a politician or bureaucrat takes notice of us. Martial law may not be in force, but it's cold comfort when the government claims—and actively exercises—the authority to indefinitely detain

U.S. citizens without providing them a day in court or outright assassinate them when they happen to be on foreign soil. Eugenics sounds like something from a totalitarian state, and yet until just a few decades ago it was commonplace in the United States. At one point, over thirty states had laws on the books dealing with varying forms of compulsory sterilization, in addition to prohibitions on interracial marriage.[3] The United States of America has slowly degraded from a values-based Republic into a despotic democracy about which voters are either ignorant, indifferent, or afraid.

Ironically, the very reasons why so many people are afraid of the government are due to policies and programs that were created and enforced with public support based, in part, upon fear. The purported threat of future terrorist attacks gives government license to read our emails, listen to our conversations, monitor our electronic data, harvest our financial records, and otherwise invade any aspect of our once-private lives. The exercise of this despotic power has startled many Americans who now have increased reason to fear the government, especially after the revelations brought to light by the Edward Snowden leaks. The fear of criminal activity has, over the decades, led the public to support an endless stream of new prohibitions, producing a voluminous set of laws that criminalize all sorts of human behavior. The results are tragic: the United States "imprisons more people—both per capita and in absolute terms—than any other nation in the world, including Russia, China and Iran"[4]; the cost of the federal prison system alone "has increased by 1,700 percent in the last three decades"[5], contributing to overall costs of the criminal justice system which exceed $200 billion annually[6]; and alarmingly, the average American citizen commits three felonies every day.[7] All of this seems to fulfill a quote by Ayn Rand:

> There's no way to rule innocent men. The only power government has is the power to crack down on criminals. Well, when there aren't enough criminals, one makes them.

One declares so many things to be a crime that it becomes impossible for men to live without breaking laws.[8]

It's rational to fear a government that uses your own money to employ a phalanx of prosecutors who, with a bit of time and creativity, could conjure up charges against you for something you did without knowing it was a crime. More alarmingly, this same government, on the loosest of pretenses, can take your children from you under a set of laws in which parents are presumed guilty until proven innocent of alleged abuse or neglect. Concerned parents around the country now fear an encounter with the child protective services agency in their state, or even losing custody of their children, for doing things as benign as letting them go for a walk[9], allowing them to play at a playground unattended[10]; or demanding a say in their medical care.[11] Due to a longstanding and irrational societal fear regarding the use of drugs, families are also traumatized through the government's "war on drugs"—more appropriately termed "war on citizens"—with over $2.5 trillion being spent to investigate, arrest, and incarcerate individuals who consume substances the state has decided to ban. Enforcing these laws often entails no-knock warrants, often served at night, leading to hysteria and confusion as homeowners (who are often innocent of the alleged crime) assume they're being invaded by armed criminals and act to protect themselves. Worse still, officers often end up invading the wrong home, thereby terrorizing completely innocent families. Victims in these situations routinely affirm a newfound distrust in the police and the government generally, along with an enduring state of fear and anxiety.

Despite so many reasons to fear the government, most people remain gullible enough to believe that same government's claims regarding any new threat. A largely compliant media conveys these claims, without context or skepticism, to the heavily propagandized public. Thus many sheep who consider their shepherd to be a little scary are nevertheless willing to follow him wherever he goes.

Fortunately, there is still time to help them overcome their fears and act boldly in defense of liberty. "The sheep of the country do not realize how loud they could sound," wrote Judge Napolitano, "if they banded together and voiced their displeasure with their shepherds. If they did, they would have a much greater effect than the lone wolf howling in the night."[12] Of course, mere howling—in other words, complaining, petitioning, protesting, etc.—is not enough. Actions speak louder than words.

As the Nazi campaign against Jews commenced and escalated, incessant propaganda led the public to believe that Jews were *Untermenschen*—subhuman. A recurrent theme in this effort to shift popular opinion was that Jews spread diseases; a popular poster published in Poland in March 1941 read, "Jews are lice; they cause typhus."[13] When the extermination phase began, many people in surrounding countries provided material support and refuge to Jews, helping them evade their would-be captors[14]; hundreds of thousands of Jews were saved through these defiant acts. Sometimes, individuals acted of their own accord to save a few lives, such as Miep Gies, a Dutch citizen, who helped hide Anne Frank, her family, and four other Jews from the Nazis. In other cases, religious leaders intervened. When Germans demanded a list of the estimated 275 Jews living on the Greek island of Zakynthos, the local Bishop returned a list that had only two names: his own, and the mayor's. Pope Pius XII opened the Vatican as a sanctuary to the Jews living in Rome. In other cases, government agents used (or exceeded) their authority by assisting in the effort. Perhaps the most notable example is that of Carl Lutz and Raoul Wallenberg, diplomats from the governments of Switzerland and Sweden, respectively. Working in parallel, they saved tens of thousands of Jews by providing them with protective letters that enabled their safe passage out of Nazi-occupied Hungary.

These and many other heroic non-Germans disbelieved and actively worked against Nazi propaganda regarding the Jewish people. Perhaps even more impressive are the stories of German citizens who protected Jews, as these individuals had to first reject the exploitation of fear that was so prevalent within their own country, and then overcome the very real fear of punishment for defying the ruling regime. Oskar Schindler, whose story was popularized in the seminal film *Schindler's List*, was a member of the Nazi party and a spy who provided intelligence to the German government. His factory employed over a thousand Jews whose deportation and death he personally prevented by repeatedly bribing Nazi officials with black-market purchases, which eventually consumed his entire fortune. Albert Göring, younger brother of the high-ranking Nazi propagandist Hermann Göring, was a German businessman who worked with the resistance and helped Jews flee concentration camps or evade Nazi capture by forging his brother's signature or otherwise invoking his family name. Berthold Beitz, tasked by the Nazis to supervise an oil refinery in Poland, used his position to fabricate jobs for hundreds of Jews, thereby helping them to avoid extermination by Germany. "I saw how people were shot, how they were lined up in the night," Beitz commented four decades after the war. "My motives were not political; they were purely humane, moral motives."[15]

A disease cannot be diagnosed, let alone treated, without first understanding its symptoms. The symptoms of fear in politics are everywhere evident for those who have eyes to see. While they may be more subtle now than during times of extreme conflict, they are no less prevalent. Practitioners of political medicine—truth tellers— are needed to help patients recognize these symptoms for what they are and properly diagnose the disease as the longstanding conformity of one's life to a narrative based on manufactured and exploited fear. In other words, people need help realizing that they have been following the wrong shepherd.

After diagnosis should come the treatment—and this book offers only general guidance as to how that should occur in the form of a few basic steps. First, a person must develop a healthy skepticism of those in power—a constant awareness that those who have been entrusted with authority have the potential to abuse it. This skepticism, however, is only the initial step on a path towards liberty. The philosopher Immanuel Kant explains:

> Skepticism is thus a resting-place for human reason, where it can reflect upon its dogmatic wanderings and make survey of the region in which it finds itself, so that for the future it may be able to choose its path with more certainty. But it is no dwelling-place for permanent settlement.[16]

Skepticism towards "official" or popular sources of information allows us to observe the media landscape more objectively and then judiciously determine who is worthy of our trust. Trust—the second step in treating the disease—is important, but it should be cautiously extended only to those who have proven themselves worthy of it. Winning an election, being appointed to a powerful position, or winning an award does not constitute a sufficient reason to be trusted. This point is especially important, as we live in a society that has prospered through the division of labor. We can't all be investigative journalists, interviewing witnesses and poring over documents in search of the truth about every story. We rely, therefore, on others to do this work for us, freeing up our time to pursue other endeavors—but we should be very discriminating when it comes to what sources we believe. We often rely upon trusted brands and vetted processes for food that will be healthy for our bodies and free of any poisons or diseases that will harm them. The same approach should be taken with what we allow into our minds. Just as we would avoid food from a company that had a reputation for selling contaminated products, we should avoid political or media figures who lie, or who fail to acknowledge or investigate the lies told by others. Conversely, we should actively support the work of trusted sources—especially when there is risk involved in their efforts to combat propaganda and reveal the truth.

The third step in treating the disease of fear is to consume a large amount of information—and to diversify our sources. In generations past, people would get their news largely from a single source: the morning newspaper, or an evening television broadcast. This captive audience became a gullible one; if readers or viewers were told to fear something, then they likely would. In our day, thanks to the internet, we have a decentralization of inputs—numberless sources of information that we can utilize to better sift through the lies and deceptions. If American media outlets are unwilling to tell the truth about something that incriminates the government, then we can easily explore what international establishments have to say. When a previously trusted news source turns out to be compromised, we have plenty of other options. Propaganda is pervasive; expanding our sources of information reduces the likelihood that politicians and pundits will be able to deceive us.

Fourth, truth-seekers must become truth-tellers. Obtaining reliable information may benefit us individually, but it becomes more effective when spread widely to others who have not yet encountered it. In epidemiology there's a concept known as herd immunity theory—the idea that the total effect of a contagious disease is reduced when the chain of infection is disrupted by immunizing a large percentage of the population. As more people become resistant, the likelihood that others will become infected is reduced. The same concept applies to fear: its potential for exploitation is significantly undermined when a large percentage of the population recognizes the hobgoblin for what it is. Determining the truth is important for our own sake, but we can have a much greater impact if we help to inoculate a large percentage of the public against the rampant disease of manufactured fear.

Finally, we should internalize and institutionalize the Golden Rule, treating others as we would want them to treat us. Whether the person be our neighbor, fellow church-goer, a member of the rival sports team, a person from an ethnic minority group, or a citizen from another country with whom we share little in common, that person is somebody with rights, interests, family members who love and depend on them, life goals, and other things common to each of us. While others work to demonize and dehumanize them, we should let love become the basis of our feelings and thoughts towards others—even, and perhaps especially, those who are being painted with broad brushes by a government looking to implement policies that will harm them.

We live in a dangerous world, and threats abound: nemesis nations, debilitating diseases, or even the common crook can disrupt or destroy a previously stable and enjoyable life. Rational people will try to mitigate threats to the extent possible, but they will focus on the pursuit of their happiness, rather than being incapacitated by fear. They recognize and reject the irrational fear of hobgoblins, no matter how often they're mentioned in the media. They understand the value of freedom and that the sea of liberty, while tempestuous at times, is well worth navigating.

NOTES

1. "Indictment of Socialism No. 3," *Barnhill-Tichenor Debate on Socialism* (St. Louis, The National Rip-Saw Publishing Co., 1914), 34.

2. "37% of Voters Fear the Federal Government," Rasmussen Reports, April 18, 2014, accessed August 2, 2014, http://www.rasmussenreports.com/public_content/politics/general_politics/april_2014/37_of_voters_fear_the_federal_government.

3. Paul A. Lombardo, *A Century of Eugenics in America: From the Indiana Experiment to the Human Genome Era* (Indiana University Press, 2011), ix.

4. "High US incarceration rate begins to decline," *The Florence Reminder & Blade-Tribune*, May 29, 2014.

5. "DOJ Says Soaring Prison Costs Hurt Criminal Justice System, Calls For Sentencing Reform" *The Huffington Post*, July 11, 2013, accessed August 2, 2014, http://www.huffingtonpost.com/2013/07/11/federal-sentencing-reform_n_3581546.html.

6. "Inside Criminal Justice," The Crime Report, June 24, 2013, accessed August 2, 2014, http://www.thecrimereport.org/news/inside-criminal-justice/2013-06-measuring-justice.

7. See Harvey Silverglate, *Three Felonies A Day: How the Feds Target the Innocent* (New York: Encounter Books, 2011).

8. Rand, *Atlas Shrugged*, 404.

9. "Florida mother arrested for neglect after letting seven-year-old son walk alone to park 800 metres away," *National Post*, July 31, 2014, accessed August 2, 2014, http://news.nationalpost.com/2014/07/31/florida-mother-arrested-for-neglect-after-letting-seven-year-old-son-walk-alone-to-park-800-metres-away/.

10. "Mom arrested for leaving 9-year-old alone at park," CNN, July 21, 2014, accessed August 2, 2014, http://www.cnn.com/2014/07/21/living/mom-arrested-left-girl-park-parents/.

11. "Parents of Sick Teen Justina Pelletier, Accused of Verbally Abusing Hospital Staff, Lose Custody," ABC News, March 26, 2014, accessed

August 2, 2014, http://abcnews.go.com/Health/parents-sick-teen-justina-pelletier-accused-verbally-abusing/story?id=23067247.

12. Napolitano, *A Nation of Sheep*, 18.

13. "Prologue: Roots of the Holocause," The Holocaust Chronicle, accessed August 2, 2014, http://www.holocaustchronicle.org/staticpages/40.html.

14. See "Individuals and groups assisting Jews during the Holocaust," Wikipedia, http://en.wikipedia.org/wiki/Individuals_and_groups_assisting_Jews_during_the_Holocaust.

15. "Berthold Beitz, German Steel Industrialist Who Saved Jews, Dies at 99," *The New York Times*, August 1, 2013, accessed August 2, 2014, http://www.nytimes.com/2013/08/02/business/berthold-beitz-german-steel-industrialist-who-saved-jews-dies-at-99.html.

16. Immanuel Kant, *Immanuel Kant's Critique of Pure Reason* (New York: Macmillan & Co., Ltd., 1963), 607.

INDEX

ABOUT THE AUTHOR

Connor Boyack is founder and president of Libertas Institute, a libertarian think tank in Utah. In that capacity, he has spearheaded important policy reforms dealing with property rights, civil liberties, transparency, surveillance, and education freedom.

He is the author of several books, including the Tuttle Twins series that teaches the principles of liberty to young children. Other books include *Latter-day Liberty: A Gospel Approach to Government and Politics* and its companion, *Latter-day Responsibility: Choosing Liberty through Personal Accountability*.

Connor's work has been publicly praised by many nationally recognized figures, and he frequently appears in local, national, and international interviews to publicize and comment on his work.

Connor lives in Utah with his wife and two children.

Find all of Boyack's books for sale at LibertasUtah.org/shop/